THE SCIENCE OF EDUCATION

THE SCIENCE OF EDUCATION

BY

THOMAS J. McEVOY

Price, Two Dollars

T. J. McEVOY, Publisher
Flatbush and Third Aves.
Brooklyn, N. Y.
1911

McEVOY PEDAGOGICAL SERIES.

McEvoy's Epitome of History and
    Principles of Education...........$1.00
McEvoy's Methods in Education..... 1.50
McEvoy's Science of Education..... 2.00
McEvoy's Answers in Methods of
    Teaching (*Four Books*)........... 6.00
McEvoy's Answers in School Manage-
    ment 1.50
McEvoy's Answers in History and
    Principles of Education (*in prepara-
    tion*). ....

PULIS PRINTING COMPANY,
BROOKLYN, N. Y.

CONTENTS

PREFACE TO SECOND EDITION.

Classification is the aim of this book. The various aspects of education are fully discussed and many lines of investigation are adequately treated in other books, but not enough authoritative work has been done to bring the leading opinions together in one satisfactory conception of all that education implies. This second edition is a contribution to the desired harmonization of thought.

The terms science of education and art of education have been commonly used as synonyms for theory and practice. But science and theory are not synonymous; science connotes an acceptable classification of data or facts, while theory may still remain within the realm of doubt. Art means aptness or skill in the use of facts scientifically classified. In this book the science of education includes both science and art as here defined, because the validity of formal classification cannot be established without the test of direct application in teaching. Failure to apply as in classroom work is the most serious defect in pedagogical study.

No argument except the book as a whole is offered to prove that there is a science of education, nor is any apology made for the effort to help students in the logical organization of thought. One safe conclusion is given under each topic for the purpose of having a viewpoint for acceptance or modification after due investigation and reflection. Lazy students may use the book as a short cut, but it is hoped that the material will serve as a stimulus to diligent minds.

The nature of this work necessarily means obligation to many associates, authors and publishers. Grateful acknowledgment is expressed for every source of help in making this SCIENCE OF EDUCATION.

THE SCIENCE OF EDUCATION

CHAPTER I

THE MEANING OF EDUCATION

1. A clear definition of education should be the first attainment in the study of the science of education. It may not be possible to find or to construct a definition which is acceptable to all educators, but it is within our power to establish a standard of thought in harmony with those who are competent to pass judgment upon such matters. This chapter has material enough to enable students to reach a safe conclusion.

Meaning from Etymology

2. The word education is derived from the Latin *educare*, to rear or nourish, and *educere*, to lead forth or draw out. This derivation is suggestive but it does not furnish an adequate definition. The present use of the term expresses the original meaning enlarged by the cumulative viewpoints of advancing civilization.

Meaning from History of Education

3. **Oriental nations.**—For the aims, purposes or conceptions of education in oriental nations, see

McEvoy's *Epitome of History and Principles of Education*, pages 6 to 25. Following is a summary:

China: Success in this life.

India: Preparation for future life.

Phoenicia: Commercial supremacy.

Persia: Service to the state

Egypt: Supremacy of priests.

Israel: Rehabilitation of the nation.

4. **Ideals in western civilization.**—Seven valuable conceptions of education are found in the history of the western nations. These conceptions are spoken of as ideals because they express so much that is worthy of acceptance. Following are the respective ideals:

CULTURE—Athens.

EFFICIENCY—Rome.

DISCIPLINE—Middle Ages, humanists, Locke.

KNOWLEDGE—Comenius, Bacon and others.

DEVELOPMENT—Rousseau, Pestalozzi, Froebel.

CHARACTER—Herbart.

CITIZENSHIP—Horace Mann, John Dewey.

5. **Our use of these ideals.**—Destructive criticism might show the inadequacy of each of these ideals as understood by the people who used them in the line of historic development of education, but an effort to interpret them as positive contribution is more in harmony with the trend of scholarly research Education itself is constructive; and surely the triumph of modern classification is not lessened by giving due credit for achievements of the past.

In attempting to make a brief exposition or a

satisfactory definition of education, what points
are serviceable in an outline? Or if we are asked
to tell specifically what aims should be in mind as
successful teachers carry on their daily work, we
may turn at once to the seven ideals that stand
for the best in more than two thousand years of
human development. It is permissible, of course,
to argue that any one, such as character, includes
the other six, but it is conducive to breadth and
organization of thought to show that each of the
seven is a worthy element in effectual education.

6. **Scope of education enlarged.**—The history
of mental movements prior to the great renaissance
is the province of history and principles of education, but attention should be directed here to the
scope of education before the sixteenth century.

Under culture as an ideal in Athens, both theory
and practice became definite enough to make education synonymous with the welfare of the people.
A theory of education is found in Plato's books,
Republic and *Laws*, and in the writings of Aristotle;
an elementary course of study, known as Music and
Gymnastics, was formulated; and methods of
teaching received permanent contributions, the
maieutic method of Socrates and the deductive
method of Aristotle. Plato's theory of ideas and
Aristotle's discussion of the inductive method deserve special consideration.

Efficiency was the Roman ideal. Organization
was made the dominant characteristic in home,
school and state. The relation of practical results
to definite aim and procedure still suggests Roman

theory and application.   Compare modern voca-
tional training.

The Middle Ages exalted discipline as an ideal.
The work of preserving education at all was a difficult task in that formative period, but the ideal
was sustained and the organization of education as
an institution was strongly established   The mo-
nastic course of study, The Seven Liberal Arts,
guided instruction for a thousand years, universities were established with faculties in Law, Medicine, Philosophy and Theology; and the early
years of scholasticism perfected the syllogism as
a method of teaching.

7. **Realism in modern education.**—The sixteenth century was characterized by realism in education.   That large tendency favored the vitalizing of all education by interpreting the lives of the
Greeks and Romans, by using French and German,
and by studying matter directly related to life.
See *Epitome*, page 132

8. **Innovation.**—The   changes   suggested   by
realism   caused   the   seventeenth   century   to   be
known as the period of the innovators.   Note the
continued effort to adjustment in mental and physical life.   See *Epitome*, page 148.

9. **Naturalism.**—The   eighteenth   century   tried
to reconcile educational theory and practice with
external physical nature and the nature of children.
See *Epitome*, page 172.

10. **Psychological, scientific, and sociological
tendencies.**—These three tendencies are strong in
modern education   By some, they are called prod-

ucts of evolution in education; by others, they are treated as phases of an eclectic view of education. We may use the three terms to characterize approved efforts to make education satisfy the needs of mankind. The historic development of each is briefly given.

Naturalism directed attention to the laws of the physical world and the inherent characteristics of children. Direct application was evidenced in the books of Rousseau and the teaching of Pestalozzi and Froebel. The psychological interpretation of facts and conditions was Herbart's contribution to education; and the immediate result was improvement in methods of teaching. Recall general method or formal steps of instruction.

The scientific movement affected subject-matter, thus modifying courses of study. Spencer's *Education*, representative of this tendency, affected methods of teaching as well as subject-matter.

The sociological movement necessitated institutional application. Compare Butler's definition of education in section 68.

Meaning from Definitions of Education

11. ARISTOTLE. The true aim of education is the attainment of happiness through perfect virtue.

12. BAGLEY. The process by means of which the individual acquires experiences that will function in rendering more efficient his future action.

13. BALDWIN. How to make the most of one's self, is not this the purpose and problem of educa-

tion? Education in its broadest sense means development. It is the evolution of every human power.

14. BROOKS. The true object of education is the perfection of the individual.

15. BRUMBAUGH. The effort of society to impress its ideals upon the thought and activity of the young.

16. COMPAYRE. Education is the sum of the reflective efforts by which we aid nature in the development of the physical, intellectual, and moral faculties of man, in view of his perfection, his happiness, and his social destination.

17. COMENIUS. Education is the development of the whole man.

18. DAVIDSON. Conscious evolution.

19. DENZEL. Education is the harmonious development of the physical, intellectual, and moral faculties.

20. DEWEY. Education is the process of remaking experience, giving it a more socialized value through increased individual experience, by giving the individual better control over his own powers.

21. EMERSON. The end of education is to train away all impediment, and to leave only pure power.

22. FICHTE. Moral culture is pre-eminently the aim of all education.

23. FROEBEL. Education shall be, essentially, a work of liberty and spontaneity.

24. FROEBEL. The object of education is the

realization of a faithful, pure, inviolate, and hence holy life.

25. ASA GRAY. To learn how to observe and how to distinguish things correctly is the greater part of education.

26. HAMILTON. The primary principle of education is the determination of the pupil to self-activity.

27. HERBART. The development of moral character.

28. HERBART. The end of education is to produce a well-balanced and many-sided interest.

29. HEWITT. The leading out and training of all the powers whose germs the child possesses at birth.

30. JAMES. To make useful habits automatic.

31. JAMES. Education is the organization of acquired habits of action such as will fit the individual to his physical and social environment.

32. JEVONS. The true view of education is to regard it as a course of training. The youth in a gymnasium practises upon the horizontal bar, in order to develop his muscular powers generally; he does not intend to go on posturing upon horizontal bars all through life. School is a place where the mental fibres are to be exercised, trained, expanded, developed and strengthened.—In *Mind*, pp. 197-207, No. VI., April, 1877.

33. JOLY. Education is the sum of the efforts, whose purpose is to give to man the complete possession and correct use of his different faculties.

34. KANT. Education is the development in man of all the perfection which his nature permits.

35. KEITH   The change in the sequence or the character of one's mental activities.

36. LOCKE   To form a perfect gentleman

37. LOCKE. The attainment of a sound mind in a sound body is the end of education.

38. MARION. Education is the sum of the intentional actions, by means of which man attempts to raise his fellow man to perfection.

39. JAMES MILL   The aim of education is to render the individual, as much as possible, an instrument of happiness to himself, and, next, to other beings.

40. JOHN STUART MILL. Education includes whatever we do for ourselves and whatever is done for us by others, for the express purpose of bringing us nearer to the perfection of our nature.

41. MILTON   A complete and generous education fits a man to perform justly, skilfully, and magnanimously all the offices, both public and private, of peace and war

42. MONTAIGNE   Education is the art of forming men, not specialists.

43. NIEMEIER   Education is at once the art and the science of guiding the young and of putting them in a condition, by the aid of instruction, through the power of emulation and good example, to attain the triple end assigned to man by his religious, social, and national destination

44. ORCUTT. Education is not the storing of knowledge, but the development of power

45. PAGE. The conclusions of the honest and intelligent inquirer after the truth in this matter, will be something like the following:—That education (from *c* and *duco*, to lead forth) is development; that it is not instruction merely—knowledge, facts, rules—communicated by the teacher, but it is discipline, it is a waking up of the mind, a growth of the mind,—growth by a healthy assimilation of wholesome aliment. It is an inspiring of the mind with a thirst for knowledge, growth, enlargement,—and then a disciplining of its powers so far that it can go on to educate itself. It is the arousing of the child's mind to think, without thinking for it; it is the awakening of its powers to observe, to remember, to reflect, to combine. It is not a cultivation of the memory to the neglect of everything else; but it is a calling forth of all the faculties into harmonious action. If to possess facts simply is education, then an encyclopaedia is better educated than a man.—*Theory and Practice of Teaching.*

46. PARKER. The realization of all the possibilities of human growth and development.

47. PARKER. The end of education is community life.

48. PAYNE. Comprehends all the influences which operate on the human being, stimulating his faculties to action, forming his habits, moulding his character, and making him what he is.

49. PESTALOZZI. The natural, progressive, and systematic development of all the powers and faculties of the human being.

50. PLATO. To give to the body and to the soul all the beauty and all the perfection of which they are capable.

51. RAAB. Education, in its broadest sense, seems to be a full, perfect discipline not only of the mental and moral powers, but of the physical as well.

52. ROARK Right education is such a preparation of the individual, in physical, intellectual and moral capacities, as will enable him to secure the highest enjoyment from their use, here and hereafter.

53. ROSENKRANZ. Education is the influencing of man by man, and it has for its end to lead him to actualize himself through his own efforts. . . . It is the nature of education only to assist in the producing of that which the subject would strive most earnestly to develop for himself if he had a clear idea of himself . . . Man, therefore, is the only fit subject for education. We often speak, it is true, of the education of plants and animals; but even when we do so, we apply, unconsciously, perhaps, other expressions, as 'raising' and 'training,' in order to distinguish these. . . . Education cannot create: it can only help to develop to reality the previously existent possibility· it can only help to bring forth to light the hidden life — *Pedagogics as a System*, 7-22, ed. 1872.

54. ROUSSEAU Education is the art of bringing up children and of forming men.

55. RUSKIN. Advancement in life.

56. SALISBURY. A process of gradual unfold-ment, the opening out of all the soul's powers.

57. SCOTT. Acquiring habits of firm and assid-uous application, and gaining the art of controlling, directing, and concentrating the powers of the mind for earnest investigations.

58. SIMON. The process by which one mind forms another mind, and one heart another heart.

59. STEIN. Education is the harmonious and equable evolution of the human faculties, by a method founded upon the nature of the mind, for developing all the faculties of the soul, for stirring up and nourishing all the principles of life, while shunning all one-sided culture and taking account of the sentiments on which the strength and worth of men depend.

60. SULLY. Education seeks, by social stimu-lus, guidance, and control, to develop the natural powers of the child, so as to render him able and disposed to lead a hearty, happy, and morally worthy life.

61. THIRY. The end of education is triple: (1) To develop the mental factulties, (2) to communi-cate knowledge, and (3) to mould character.

62. THORNDIKE. The work of education is to make changes in human minds and bodies.

63. THORNDIKE. To give boys and girls health in body and mind, information about the world of nature and men, worthy interests in knowledge and action, a multitude of habits of thought, feeling, and behavior, and ideals of efficiency, honor, duty, love and service.

64. TOMPKINS   That power and versatility of thought and emotion which elevate life into truth and virtue.

65. WARD.   Education means the universal distribution of extant knowledge.

66. WHITE   Education is any process or act which results in knowledge or power or skill.

DEFINITIONS FOR INTENSIVE STUDY

67. Eclectic conception of education.—An acceptable definition of education is eclectic, *i. e.*, a combination of the best features of all other definitions.   Such a definition embodies the cumulative merits as merits are determined by modern needs. Study the following definitions, abstract the essentials, and then construct a definition satisfactory to yourself.   If you consider one of these definitions adequate, prepare to defend that one.   Can you show that sections 68 to 75, inclusive, give an eclectic conception of education embodying the best thought in all of the foregoing definitions?

68. Adaptation to spiritual inheritance.—BUTLER.   If education cannot be identified with mere instruction, what is it?   What does the term mean? I answer, it must mean a gradual adjustment to the spiritual possessions of the race   Those possessions are at least fivefold   The child is entitled to his scientific inheritance, to his literary inheritance, to his aesthetic inheritance, to his institutional inheritance and to his religious inheritance

69. Participation in social consciousness of the

race.—DEWEY. The increasing participation of the individual in the social life of the race. All education proceeds by the participation of the individual, in the social consciousness of the race. . . . The school is a form of community life in which the child shares the inherited resources of the race, and uses his own powers for social ends. Education is, therefore, a process of living and not a preparation for future living.

70. **Social fitness.**—HARRIS (*a*) The process by which the individual man lifts himself to the species (*b*) The preparation of the individual for reciprocal union with society

71. **Self-realization.** — HORNE Self-development through self-activity for self-hood and social service

72. **Character and social efficiency.**—MAXWELL. What does "education for efficiency" mean? It does not mean that every man should be trained to be a soldier. True, the man who is well trained for the duties of peace is, in these days of scientific instruments of destruction, well prepared for war, but military prowess can never become the ideal of education among a great industrial people. It does not mean merely that each citizen should be able to read the newspapers and magazines, so that he may be familiar with political discussions, and able to make an intelligent choice between candidates and policies The imparting of such knowledge to each individual is essential in a democratic nation, but it falls far short of the education needed to secure the highest efficiency of each unit of society. Still less

does it mean that wretched travesty of education
which would confine the work of the public schools
to those exercises in reading, writing, and ciphering
which will enable a boy or a girl, at the age of fourteen or earlier, to earn starvation wages in a store
or factory. Education for efficiency means all of
these things; but it means much more. It means
the development of each citizen, first as an individual, and second as a member of society. It means
bodies kept fit for service by appropriate exercise.
It means that each student shall be taught to use
his hands deftly, to observe accurately, to reason
justly, to express himself clearly. It means that he
shall learn "to live cleanly, happily, and helpfully,
with those around him," that he shall learn to co-
operate with his fellows for far-reaching and far-
distant ends, that he shall learn the everlasting
truth of the words uttered nearly two thousand
years ago: "No man liveth to himeslf," and, "Bear
ye one another's burdens " Such, I take it, is the
goal of American education —*President's Address,
N. E. A.,* 1904.

73. **Harmonization.**—MONROE.   The harmonization of interest and effort.

74. **Complete living.**—SPENCER   Complete living is the end of education. We must not simply
think but know what information will be useful in
after-life. The activities, which constitute human
life, may be classified in the order of their importance: (1) Direct self-preservation, (2) indirect
self-preservation; (3) the rearing of children; (4)

social demands and citizenship; (5) miscellaneous
activities filling the leisure part of life.

75. **Meeting of the minds.**—WOODROW WIL-
SON. Education is a process—a process of life, of
development under a score of influences, chiefly
personal. Education is not a process of instruction,
but comes by the intimate daily contacts of im-
mature minds with minds more mature and experienced.

For Study

76. **Interpretation.**—The breadth suggested by
the study of so many definitions presupposes considerable intensive study of the meaning of education. The attempt to interpret fifty definitions
loses its disciplinary value if students are groping
for a guiding thought. Better go at once to sections 67 to 75 for a safe foundation, learn one definition, such as Butler's, and then strengthen that
conception by comparing it with other definitions,
such as Spencer's. If vagueness accompanies the
comparison, evidently the student is at the wrong
end of the process of learning; he must go back
to fundamental work. Thoughtful study of one
book is recommended; later collateral reading will
serve a purpose if needed for fixing impressions.
But the one great danger is the tendency to choose
striking expressions from many books for the purpose of combining those expressions. Don't do
that; mature scholarship cannot be deceived by
sound. Try to get one definite idea clearly expressed and then enlarge your chosen conception.

A safe foundation can be secured by using one or all of these books:

Butler's *The Meaning of Education.*
Horne's *Philosophy of Education.*
Spencer's *Education.*

Test Questions

77. Discuss *happiness*, *perfection* and *power* as aims in education.

78. Define each of the seven ideals in western civilization.

79. If you were asked to choose one of those seven ideals as a comprehensive aim or end, which one would you choose? Why?

Mention five ways in which one day of your teaching satisfies that ideal.

80. What does Butler mean by spiritual inheritance? Illustrate each of the five kinds in high school work. (See *Methods in Education*, 18).

81. What knowledge does Spencer consider of most worth? Comment on his view of the rearing of children.

82. Define social efficiency.

83. What is the meaning of eclectic? Give its derivation. Quote or make an eclectic definition of education.

84. Pythagoras made harmony the basis of his scheme of education. What modern author epitomizes education by that term? Why does he choose interest and effort?

85. Write not more than two hundred words

on the substance of the INTRODUCTION to Horne's
Philosophy of Education

86. Express in one line the essential thought in
Wilson's definition in section 75.

87. References.—These books are given to
guide general reading, but no student is expected
to try to master all of them

BAGLEY   *Educative Process.*
BAIN.   *Education as a Science*
DEGARMO.   *Interest and Education.*
DEWEY.   *School and Society*
ELIOT.   *Educational Reform*
FROEBEL.   *Education of Man.*
GORDY   *A Broader Elementary Education*
HANUS.   *Educational Aims and Values*
HARRIS.   *Psychologic Foundations of Education*
HERBART.   *Outlines of Educational Doctrine.*
HILL.   *True Order of Studies.*
HILLIS.   *A Man's Value to Society.*
HORNE   *The Psychological Principles of Education*
MONROE   *Brief Course in History of Education*
O'SHEA.   *Dynamic Factors in Education.*
O'SHEA.   *Education as Adjustment.*
PESTALOZZI.   *Leonard and Gertrude*
Report of Committee of Fifteen.
Report of Committee of Ten.
Report of Committee of Twelve
ROUSSEAU.   *Emile.*
SEELEY   *Elementary Pedagogy.*
SEARCH.   *Ideal School.*
TOMPKINS.   *Philosophy of Education*
WILSON.   *Pedagogues and Parents,*

CHAPTER II

ASPECTS OF EDUCATION

88. Bases.—Horne's *Philosophy of Education* presents a comprehensive discussion of education under five aspects. Biological, physiological, sociological, psychological, and philosophical. These aspects are called phases or bases by some writers.

89. Means of approach.—The general study of education may be approached through the history of education, the science of education, applied principles or practice of education, and the philosophy of education.

90. Continuity of the process; the school a social institution.—The classifications mentioned in 88 and 89 are not indications of distinct processes in education; they are rather convenient ways of considering one large unity. All the agencies or factors—the school, the home, the church, the vocation, and the state—are brought into harmony in producing the desired results. This thought is well expressed in section 91 by a quotation from Mac-Vannel's *Syllabus of Philosophy of Education*, p. 48.

91. MacVannel quoted.—"The educative process is essentially continuous. The idea fundamental to the process is the realization of the individual through his increasing participation in the knowledge, the interests and activities of social life.

From the individual's earliest infancy this process of participation has been widening and deepening, and always to some degree under the direction and control of the expectations and demands of those who form the social enclosure of his life. Family life no matter how unorganized it may at first sight appear, saturates the child's mind, directs his activity and thus introduces some degree of order into his unregulated impulses. In the school is found a more highly organized factor in the process of mediating the fund of social interests and values and thus securing the social transformation of the individual. Yet while the school as a moral institution may perform its task more consciously or more systematically than the family or the other educative institutions, it cannot do so more inevitably or with more permanent or far-reaching effect. The entire environment of the individual as concentrated in the great human institutions, the home, the school, the vocation, the state, and the church, is to be regarded fundamentally as a medium in which the educational process, as a unitary and continuous thing, is organized and directed. The school, therefore, is that form of institutional life in which are concentrated those agencies and influences through which society endeavors to reinforce the life of those who are to be its members with such forms of experience as make for effective membership in a social order."—*Extension Syllabi, Series A. No. 12, Teachers' College, Columbia University.*

92. **Dewey quoted.**—"I believe that the individual who is to be educated is a social individuual,

and that society is an organic union of individuals.
If we eliminate the social factor from the child we
are left only with an abstraction; if we eliminate
the individual factor from society, we are left only
with an inert lifeless mass.   Education, therefore,
must begin with a psychological insight into the
child's capacities, interests, and habits.   It must be
controlled at every point by reference to these same
considerations.   These powers, interests, and habits
must be continually interpreted—we must know
what they mean.   They must be translated into
terms of their social equivalents—into terms of
what they are capable of in the way of social service."—*Educational Creeds*, p. 8.

93.   **Gordy's criticism of Dewey.**—"Now, in criticising this definition I do not wish to be understood
as disagreeing with it.   On the contrary, I wish at
the outset to say that I regard it as asserting by
implication a very important truth, that the true
interest of the individual and that of society are
identical   My criticism of the definition is that it
does not tell us in what the interests either of the
individual or of society are to be found   To be told
that the interests of the individual are the same as
those of society tells me nothing unless I know what
the interests of society are.   To be told that the interests of society are the same as those of the individual leaves me entirely in the dark unless I
know what the interests of the individual are.   The
teacher has to deal with a lot of psychological raw
material, and he wishes to know what he shall try
to make of it, toward what ideal he shall seek to

have it shape itself. Is it not evident that the one
thing that he needs to know is in what the true interests of the individual lie? And is it not equally
clear that you are giving him no positive conception
when you tell him that the interests of the individual consist in such a development of his powers
as will enable him to see and respond to the interests of society? I say, no positive conception: there
is a negative idea of very great value in Dr. Dewey's
definition. He says that the material, selfish view of
education is not the true one: so far it is good. But
when we ask for a positive statement of the end of
education, his definition gives us nothing but words.
It tells us that it consists in such a training of the
individual as will promote the interest of society.
But it does not tell us in what the interests either
of the individual or of society consists."—*A Broader
Elementary Education*, p. 70.

94. **Education from nature, men and circumstances.**—Consider this excerpt from Rousseau (a)
for its validity as an opinion, (b) for its agreement
or lack of agreement with sections 91, 92, 93.

"We are born weak, we have need of help; we are
born destitute of everything, we stand in need of
assistance; we are born stupid, we have need of
understanding. All that we are not possessed of at
our birth, and which we require when grown up, is
bestowed on us by education. This education we
receive from nature, from men, or from circumstances. The constitutional exertion of our organs
and faculties is the education of nature; the uses we
are taught to make of that exertion constitute the

education given us by men; and in the acquisitions made by our own experience, on the objects that surround us, consists our education from circumstances. We are formed, therefore, by three kinds of masters. Of these three different kinds of education, that of nature depends not on ourselves; and but in a certain degree that of circumstances; the third, which belongs to men, is that only`we have in our power: and even of this we are masters only in imagination; for who can flatter himself he will be able entirely to govern the discourse and actions of those who are about a child?"—*From Emile*.

Evolution

95. **Education an evolutionary process.**—If we claim unity, continuity and development as characteristics of the educative process, may we not say that education is an evolutionary process? Evolution in this sense is not intended to mean all that is implied in animal evolution The doctrine of evolution, as applied to lower animal life, rests upon (1) the struggle for existence, (2) the survival of the fittest, and (3) natural selection Surely the first is operative, and the other two may claim consideration in education. But analogy becomes clearer if we take adjustment to environment as a conception of education. Biologically, the word adjustment characterizes the whole struggle for physical development; and likewise in spiritual life, adjustment is both psychological and

sociological in its connotation. The adjective evolutionary may, therefore, be applied to the educative process.

For lucid treatment of this question, consult Ruediger's *The Principles of Education*, 40-56.

96. Deductions from the evolutionary conception.—The two most impressive deductions from the evolutionary method of study are, first, the continuity of existence, the *organic oneness* of all things in spite of the great contrasts in the spheres of mechanism, chemism, organism and spirit; second, that existence, so far as we know it in nature and mind, is dynamic, in a continual process of becoming. It is presupposed that the natural and social orders are parts of one organic process, and, in some way or other, form one cosmos. Man's living nature, therefore, is related to the nature of all life. In thus making man in his entire nature subject to evolutionary law an advantage is presented to the cause of education. Man is viewed as the outcome of the creative process of the world, and education becomes the last and highest form of evolution.—*MacVannel.*

97. Further analogy.—Is there anything in the process of education as a fact of our experience by means of which educational theory may be brought into definite relationship with the facts of organic and social evolution?

(*a*) In man as compared with the lower animals there is found (1) a more completely organized nervous system, (2) a more complex psychical life, (3) a corresponding lengthening of the period of

infancy. An adequate interpretation of the meaning of infancy was not forthcoming prior to the rise
of the doctrine of evolution as a scientific method.

(b) The presuppositions of the life process in
organic and social evolutions are *organism* and *environment*. In both spheres of life-process is a process of adapting the organism to its environment.

(c) Education, in its widest sense, is a process of
adaptation, made possible and necessary because
of the period of infancy in the individual, and in
this way was formed an integral part of organic
and social evolution.   The lengthening of the
period of infancy renders education at once possible and imperative.—*MacVannel*.

98. **Period of infancy.**—This expression is
used to denote the period of dependence on parental care. Growing out of and supporting the doctrine of evolution, it has been interpreted as nature's compliment to mankind   In the ascending
scale from the amoeba to man, the period of im-
maturity gradually lengthens until in the human
species alone the period of infancy is long enough
to insure the individual a development from instinctive action to rational control. The period of
infancy, being a period of plasticity, is receptive to
all the educative agencies mentioned in this chapter.

Culture Epoch Theory

99. **Meaning.**—This theory "holds that the individual in his development reproduces the main
stages passed through in the evolution of the

race; in other words, that *development* reproduces *evolution*; the educational inference being that the culture products in particular epochs in the evolution of the race are the most appropriate material for the individual in his corresponding stages of development." In other words: "The individual mind in its development repeats the order of development of the race mind." The history of civilization presents certain stages or epochs as the pastoral epoch, the nomadic epoch, the stone age, the bronze age, the hunting stage, the agricultural epoch, and so on. It is believed that each stage of race development shows certain· culture products in religion, history, literature, etc., and that such culture products should be arranged in the course of study for the corresponding epochs or stages in child development.

100. **Value.**—The chief value of the culture epoch theory is in the side light it throws upon child psychology, and in the recognition it gives to the individual's oneness with the race. It is helpful in explaining certain tendencies and impulses peculiar to children's growth. But it is doubtful whether anything of value has been or can be discovered by working comformably to the theory that might not be discovered through a sympathetic study of the individual without reference to his recapitulation of race development.

Any attempt to apply the theory closely must be futile, for only the most general correspondence can be found between the periods of the child's development and the epochs of race

growth.   Even if it were possible to establish exact correspondence, it would be unwise to plan a
course of study and methods of teaching in strict
conformity therewith, for the sufficient reason
that, in his recapitulation, the average child ex-
hibits some characteristics it is highly desirable to
eliminate.   The child, as the heir of the race,
should be put in possession of only the best which
the race has gained for him.   And he should be
trained to adapt himself to the actual conditions
of modern life, not to those of bygone eras.—
Roark, *Economy in Education*, p. 211.   See also *N. E.
A. Report*, '99:576; *Ed. Review*, 15:374; *Ed. Review*,
17:105; *Journal of Ped.*, 12:295; 16:136.

101.   **Applied in Germany.**—In Germany this
theory has been put into practice largely as an aid
in correlation.   Literature and history are chosen
for their cultural content in selecting adapted material, while manumental training is entirely ig-
nored.   The adapted course begins with myths,
passes through Robinson Crusoe, Thuringian
stories, the Niebelungen songs, the early German
history and, finally, considers the recent periods
of national development.

102.   **Not favored in America.**—In America this
theory has not been generally accepted.   The experiments that have been made here are based
upon the manumental arts in recognition of the
efforts of the race to adjust itself to its material
environment.

103.   **Recapitulation; parallelism.**—These names
are frequently applied to the culture epoch theory.

In striving to show a rigid recapitulation, many
writers are arguing for organic evolution; but our
purpose is to ascertain what biological laws can be
called into service in education to supplement our
efforts for efficiency, irrespective of the rigid parallelism which some seek to establish. We have
seen how the period of infancy permitted the substitution of plasticity and intelligence for fixity
and instinct, and we know from experience in
teaching that the undesirable tendencies (instinctive acts) of childhood can be converted into useful habits by the law of substitution Enough,
then, to encourage education to work toward desired ends according to pedagogical laws without
permitting the child to repeat the ancestral mistakes according to the strict interpretation of recapitulation. Here, again, the right of choice is the
privilege of experienced teachers

104. **Authority quoted.**—Admitting its provis-
ional character as a scientific theory, it will at
once be recognized how this idea of correspondence between race evolution and individual development would tend to emphasize the essentially organic and social character of consciousness, and
that the development of the individual must be .
along the lines marked out by the previous evolutionary process In other words, that the progress
of the future must be essentially in the directions
and by the methods indicated in the spiritual
achievements of the past.—*MacVannel*, p. 55.

Formal Discipline

105.   Meaning.—The theory of formal discipline
asserts that mental power developed in one subject
is usable in any other —Horne, *Principles,* p 66.

This theory brings up two phases of daily teaching, form and content of matter.   The historic
theory held that it does not matter what is studied,
provided it is studied rightly.   This is the doctrine
of power in education, and, as Horne says, power
applicable to any task that is assigned to us.   Modern opinion exalts content, since interest is attached to matter related to life.   The object of interest is present, not in the distant future

The argument against the theory that there are
distinct faculties in the human mind is contradicted
by modern scientific research.   Horne does not believe in rejecting the theory altogether, however,
but he would modify it and express it in this way:
"Mental power developed in one subject is applicable to any other in direct proportion to their similarity.   This principle means the greater the similarity between two subjects the greater the applicability of mental power developed in one to the
other; the less similarity, the less applicability."
(*Principles*, p. 71.)

106.   DeGarmo quoted.—"This doctrine is used
as a standing argument for so-called disciplinary
education, especially that in pure mathematics and
classical languages.   The assumption is that if the
student masters these, he will thereby acquire a
mental power that can be applied almost equally

well to any kind of practical or professional life. This gymnastic theory of education involves the idea that it does not matter upon what the mind is exercised, provided only the exercise be vigorous and long-continued. The inadequacy of the theory lies in the fact that it ignores or underestimates the importance of the choice of subjects, both for their gymnastic efficiency, and their ultimate worth in developing the individual. A life of crime develops acuteness of intellect, but it does not develop good citizens. Again, mental alertness in philology, or grammar, or higher algebra, does not insure corresponding alertness in those fields in which there is neither knowledge nor interest. The mind is never efficient in any department of endeavor in which either education or experience has not provided rich and abundant masses of apperceiving ideas."— In *Dictionary of Philosophy*.

107. **Modification suggested.**—The movements in educational criticism are likely to reach extremes Teaching without text-books sought to overcome abuse of the memory process, but the remedy was worse than the evil since pupils were made entirely dependent upon teachers. Lists of words were substituted for spelling books because the books were not adapted to all the pupils; result, an epoch of shameful misspelling Latin and Greek were taught as content studies by the absorptive method, and the students failed in freshman college work. Geometry was made inductive and the theorems were not memorized; result, quick return to a method that called memory and

reasoning into action. The prudent teacher knows that the best content must be associated with definite form. Call the practice discipline, culture or other name, as you like, but see that every child works persistently toward a habit of mastery of all rules, directions, laws, or forms that are needed as a basis for clear concepts. In higher education, too, this suggestion holds, particularly with reference to the training of the memory. False psychology need not be summoned to uphold this practice; confused concepts and incoherent language demand a remedy that can be found in consistently applying formal training to the interpretation of suitable content.

108. **Affiliated interests.**—A classification of educative activities, aside from the actual classroom work, includes athletics, literary societies, school publications, musical organizations, summer camps, nature study clubs and alumni associations. These supplementary agencies already exist; the point for consideration is how to use each agency in producing results that are desirable contributions in the work of education. See index for school fraternities.

109. **The school and the community.**—The five institutional factors in education are mentioned in section 90. An outline suggests means and values in bringing all the factors into co-operation. The topic is suggestively treated by Dutton's *School Management*, page 200. The outline given here is a composite one based on several authorities.

1. **The school and the home.**
   a. Visits by teachers and nurses.
   b. Parents' meetings.
   c. Improvement societies.
   d. School exhibitions.
   e. Rhetorical exercises.
   f. Pupils' report cards.
   g. Graduation exercises.
2. **The school and the church.**—Lines of effort parallel with those in the school and the home.
3. **The school and the state.**
   a. Obedience to law.
   b. Respect for authority.
   c. Desire to co-operate.
4. **The school and the library.**
   a. Literature and character.
   b. Desire for self-improvement.
   c. Substitution in habit: reading vs. idleness.
5. **The school and the museum.**
   a. Visualization.
   b. Recorded observation, a means of causing reactions. Notes on observations put into composition form.
   c. Collecting impulse stimulated and guided.
   d. Aesthetic influence.
6. **The school and the newspaper.**
   a. The support of the press needed.
   b. Current history a vitalizing force.
   c. School papers as means of expression.
7. **The school and industry.**

a. Excursions.

b. Commercial geography.

c. Applied arithmetic.

d. Correlation with life.

110.   **The school as a social centre.**—This phase of education is modern   Think again how to make these agencies effective.   The principle of school extension is that education is a life process.   If you agree with this principle, think of five ways in which your teaching can satisfy it.

1.   Vacation schools.

2.   Evening schools.

3.   Free lectures

4.   Parents' associations

5.   School decoration

111.   **Assignment for written work.**

1.   Name the five institutional factors in education.

2.   Is individuality necessarily sacrificed in the adjustment of the individual to society?

3.   Explain (a) social consciousness, (b) social stimulus, (c) socialization

4.   (a) State briefly the doctrine of formal discipline.   (b) Discuss its validity, citing one experiment or definite observation.   (c) What are the practical implications of the rejection and of the acceptance of this doctrine?

5.   (a) State the general doctrine of evolution and name the chief factors involved in the process. (b) Show how the educational process may be regarded as an evolution, and indicate the factors in-

volved. (c) Show in two definite aspects the bearing of the evolutionary doctrine upon educational practice.

112. **Organization.**—It is evident that organization is needed in any attempt to harmonize these various agencies in education. Psychological and sociological relationships are prominent in all the efforts to secure adjustment. Opportunity is another name for education.

CHAPTER III

THE COURSE OF STUDY

113. **Logical relation.**—In the study of the science of education, the first step is to secure a satisfactory definition of education. That definition is an aim or standard in all subsequent work. The second step is to ascertain the nature of the subject-matter to be used in trying to satisfy the general aim of education. This necessitates a consideration of the curriculum Then, having the aim and the matter, we must consider methods of teaching as the third step, and the fourth is the justification of the first three by psychological princples of education. These four steps form a large working plan in the science of education.

114. **Meaning.**

1   The epitomized representation to the child of the cultural inheritance of the race.—Monroe's *Text Book*, p. 756.

2   The spiritual organism of experience.—*Mac-Vannel*

This agrees with Monroe's definition.

3   The course of study is too often considered an objective arrangement of real things; whereas it is but the successive transformations throughout which the pupil passes in his progress towards

self-realization.—Tompkins, p. 262, *Philosophy of Teaching*.

4. For further research, consult Horne's *Philosophy of Education*, chapter V; Seeley's *Elementary Pedagogy*, chapters II, V, XVI; Butler's *Meaning of Education*, chapters I and II; *Committee of Fifteen*, page 41; *Committee of Ten*, Index I and VI; Findlay, *Principles of Class Teaching*, pages 18-52; Dewey, *My Pedagogic Creed*, and *Ethical Principles Underlying Education;* Hanus, *Educational Aims and Methods*.

115. **Principles determining course of study.**— Our conception of education embodies the reciprocal relations of the individual and society. It is not enough to know our civic duties; right thinking must pass into right action. So the first principle is a sociological one; the second, psychological. The former shows what subject-matter will tend to develop broad, useful, efficient knowledge; the latter indicates the manner of adapting the chosen subjects to the capacities of individual minds.

MacVannel writes as follows on the principles determining the selection of studies: (a) "Sociological. Does the study (as a group of facts or principles gathered together and systematized) embody some fundamental phase of social experience? Does it represent a fundamental manifestation of the spiritual life of the race? What interest is fundamental to the study? (b) Psychological. What part does the study play in helping the individual to interpret his crude experience and to control his powers with reference to social ends?—

Syllabus, 12, p. 57. See Seeley, p. 270, for further discussion.

See Seeley's *Elementary Pedagogy,* pages 20, 57 and 271 for another expression of opinion

116. **Arrangement.**—The New York City course of study is arranged according to Butler's definition of education as given in section 68. The five divisions corresponding to inheritances are in the elementary and the secondary courses. Take the exposition in the following paragraph and see if those inheritances can be traced through the high school course. Is it not advisable to add a sixth inheritance, the industrial inheritance?

The scientific inheritance is found in geography, nature study, mathematics, and physics; the literary inheritance includes all forms of literary composition and interpretation; the aesthetic inheritance includes drawing, music, and all other kinds of art that may aid in forming a higher conception of life; the institutional inheritance is found in all kinds of civic training, including political geography, history, civics, and all the subordinate forms of government represented in state and municipal organizations; and the religious inheritance includes all forms of training that are conducive to spiritual perfection.

117. **DeGarmo on arrangement**—In *Interest and Education*, page 62, DeGarmo says that "the normally constituted mind should dwell, for a time at least, upon each distinctive department of human knowledge." Then he gives us the classification as follows:

"We have first of all the *human sciences,*—those that pertain to man as man, to his life as embodied in institutions. Excluding the professional aspects of such studies, this group embraces languages, ancient and modern, literature, art, and history.

"Next we have the *natural sciences,*—those that pertain to nature as such,—they are physics, chemistry, and astronomy, together with their basis of pure mathematics; the biological sciences; and the earth sciences, like physical geography and geology.

"Finally we have the *economic sciences,*—those that show the mind of man in intimate interaction with the forces of nature. These sciences embrace economics proper, technology, and commercial knowledge and technique.

"We have here from nine to twelve distinct departments of knowledge, according to the minuteness of our classification. The social reason why every student should have something of each, is that each represents a distinct and important department of human achievement. The psychological reason why each mind should come in contact with every one of these departments, is that each one embodies a distinct method, a definite mental movement, not found adequately represented in any other branch. The method of linguistics, for instance, is quite distinct from that of mathematics or art or history. The evolutionary sciences are wholly different in method from the exact sciences. In the same way commercial technique differs from that of mechanics."

118. Dewey's opinion. — Consult *Educational Creeds*, p. 11; *School and Society*; *Ethical Principles Underlying Education*. Following is MacVannel's interpretation of Dewey's views:

Professor Dewey maintains that the education of the present must undergo, in response to the changed social conditions, a reconstruction in aim, in subject-matter and method; a reconstruction not hurried nor haphazard, but thorough-going and rational. This reconstruction, moreover, Professor Dewey holds, is already in progress. For him the controlling factors in the primary curriculum of the future are "manual training, science, nature-study, art and history. These keep alive the child's positive and creative impulses, and direct them in such ways as to discipline them into the habits of thought and action required for effective participation in community life." "It is possible to initiate the child from the first in a direct, not abstract or symbolic, way, into the operations by which society maintains its existence, material and spiritual." "The present has its claims. It is in education, if anywhere, that the claims of the present should be controlling * * *" "Nevertheless eternal vigilance is the price of liberty, and eternal care and nurture are the price of maintaining the precious conquest of the past—of preventing a relapse into Philistinism, that combination of superficial enlightenment and dogmatic crudity. If it were not for an aristocracy of the past, there would be but little worth conferring upon the democracy of to-day."

119. **Harris on arrangement.**—See *Psychologic Foundations of Education,* 321-341.

"The studies of the school will fall naturally into these five co-ordinate groups: first, mathematics and physics; second, biology, including chiefly the plant and the animal; third, literature and art, including chiefly the study of literary works of art; fourth, grammar and the technical and scientific study of language, leading to such branches as psychology; fifth, history and the study of sociological, political and social institutions. Each one of these groups should be represented in the curriculum of the schools at all times by some topic suited to the age and previous training of the pupil." (Page 323.)

Agreeing with the Committee of Fifteen, Dr. Harris places emphasis upon the spiritual dependence of the individual on the civilization into which the individual is born. His theory further emphasizes the function of the school as a means of maintaining civilization by producing types of men in harmony with the ideals of civilization; and under this view, the unity and continuity of human experience will determine the selection and the correlation of studies.

120. **Characteristics.**—Adaptability, flexibility, correlation, co-ordination, enrichment and concentration are defined as characteristics of modern courses of study.

1. Adaptability refers to the ease with which a course of study may be fitted to the needs of the community. Flexibility is a special application of

adaptability. The New York City course of study has adaptability because it satisfies the large needs of American life; the course has flexibility because it can be fitted to the special needs of sections or districts or schools in New York City

2.   Correlation of studies has reference to the organic relation of lines of thought running through the course, while enriching the course has reference to the unfolding of single lines of thought.

Correlation, then, is putting such subjects side by side at a given time in the course as will help to bring to view the universal relations involved in the study of any one of them.—Tompkins, *Philosophy of Teaching*, p 263.

For four explanations of correlation, as given by the Committee of Fifteen, see *Methods of Education*, 11.

3.   The arrangement of studies in group of equal rank is co-ordination of studies.   Illustration in plans of Butler, DeGarmo and Harris

4   Enriching the course of study is an effort to bring the elements of the higher subjects, such as geometry, general history, literature, botany and astronomy into the very beginning of the course, thereby replacing and postponing the abstruse phases of some of the lower subjects.   There is a phase of astronomy more elementary than a phase of arithmetic; and it would enrich the course to have astronomy brought down in the place of that phase of arithmetic which can make no appeal to the pupil because too abstract and general for his

concrete way of thinking.—Tompkins, *Philosophy of Teaching*, p. 262.

5. A curriculum based upon concentration of studies has one study as the centre or core, and other related studies are grouped around the core. Ziller, a disciple of Herbart, used literature and history as the core; Colonel Parker used geography; and John Dewey advocates manual training.

Concentration favors a strict interpretation of the culture epoch theory. Germany favors concentration, but America does not.

121. **Characteristics distinguished.** — Observe that concentration makes use of one central study with radiating lines of related knowledge; that co-ordination makes use of more than one study,—five in the scheme of Harris, such groups being of equal value, and that correlation utilizes the general lines of related knowledge running through and unifying all the subjects and all the groups of subjects in the course of study. Correlation is a general term including concentration and co-ordination.

122. **Roark quoted.**—"So far as definitions may be drawn from the literature of the Herbartian writers and their critics, the term 'correlation' is generic and includes the other two. 'Concentration' means the grouping or correlating of studies around a central core, between which and the other subjects some vital relation exists. 'Co-ordination' is the correlation of several groups of studies with one another, each group made up of associated subjects, and equal in rank to each other group."—*Economy in Education*, 212.

123. **Tompkins on concentration.**—The theory of "concentration" from which so much is now promised, as usually taught and practiced, is but the wavering image of the universal law of method. True concentration is not the strained and mechanical bringing together of diverse subject-matter into the same recitation, but fixing the attention on all the relations of the given subject, and thus drawing into the movement the other subjects required for the mastery of the one under consideration. In the true unifying process, emphasis must be given to the content and not to the extent of subject-matter; whereas, superficial concentration emphasizes the diversity of matter which may be disposed of during a given period. In teaching a plant, the teacher must not say to himself, "Now I must bring into the discussion geometry, literature, theology, etc.," but rather, "Now I must press the pupil's attention close to the relations which constitute the plant." If this should involve the facts and laws of geometric forms, let it be so; if this should reveal the infinite life, appealing as a poem to the sense of the beautiful, it must be well; if this should manifest infinite wisdom and supernatural power, theology has found its way into the movement without awkward circumlocution to make a place for it. If the thing be taught in the only way it can truly be taught, whatever subjects are needed will inevitably be drawn into the process.—*Tompkins*, p. 261.

124. **Application.**—The use of these characteristics in theory and practice is shown by no other man so well as by Dr. Maxwell in his address on

SOME PHASES OF THE NEW COURSE OF STUDY (1904)
The address is printed in full in *Methods in Education*,
pages 15 to 35. Students in higher education can
profitably study those basal ideas and then trace the
application of the principles through all grades in
our school system.

**125. Co-ordination beyond the elementary
school.**—Higher instruction continues on the five
lines marked out for elementary and secondary instruction, taking up such branches as (*a*) higher
mathematical studies and their applications in
physics; (*b*) the several sciences that contribute to
a knowledge of the processes of the earth and of
organic beings (geology, biology, meteorology,
etc); (*c*) ancient and modern languages, comparative philology, logic, philosophy; (*d*) political
economy and sociology, moral philosophy, philosophy of civil history, constitutional history; (*e*) philosophy and history of art, literature and rhetoric.—
Harris, *Psychologic Foundations of Education*, p. 334

126. Limitations of correlation in teaching.—
Teaching the two things to be related at the same
time is in fact not the essential in correlation, but
only one means. The essential is that the two be
related in the pupil's mind One may be taught five
years after the other, but if its relations with the
other are then made a part of the pupil's mental
equipment, all may be well. One may be taught
by one teacher and the other by another teacher,
but if each teacher makes the necessary cross-con-
nections, the two systems of connections in the
pupil's mind will henceforth co-operate.

The chief dangers to be avoided in teaching relationships are: (1) such an infatuation with the doctrine of correlation as leads one to waste time in teaching relationships so obvious that a pupil is sure to make them for himself or so trivial that they are not worth the making, and (2) such ignorance or carelessness as leads one to teach relationships that are false or artificial It is as bad or even worse to teach a useless relationship as a useless fact, a false relationship as a false fact.—Thorndike, *Principles of Teaching*, p. 129.

127. **An eclectic course of study.**—Modern courses of study are said to be eclectic because they embody the chosen culture products of civilization. To complete the five inheritances, it is suggested that a sixth, industrial inheritance, be added to satisfy the recognition of industrial training as a part of systematic education. As an interesting study in development, recall what was taught in the oriental nations and then trace the history of courses of study The following courses are suggested, with references by pages to McEvoy's *Epitome of History and Principles of Education:*

1. Greece—Music and Gymnastics, pages 38 and 58.

2. Rome—Utilitarian Tendencies, pages 60 and 70.

3 Monasticism—Seven Liberal Arts, page 86

4. Early Christian Universities—Law, Medicine, Philosophy, Theology, page 102.

5 Sturm—Classical High School Course, page 128.

6. Jesuits—Ratio Studiorum, page 130
7. Comenius—Nature, page 154.
8. Spencer—Science, page 216
9. Modern—Eclectic. See opinions of Harris, Dewey, DeGarmo, Butler, and others

128. **Suggestive exercise.**

1. Illustrate enrichment in a high school course

2   Define apperception. Show its relation to the apperceptive process   .

3   To what extent would you correlate English history and English literature? Illustrate.

4. To what extent would you correlate the study of the Latin language and the study of Roman life.

5. Can composition and chemistry be correlated? Give reason for your answer.

6. "Every recitation may be made a recitation in language " Comment upon this   Would you, for instance, teach punctuation, spelling, correct forms of speech, etc , in a regular lesson in your specialty?

7. Give reasons for or against correlating the following:

(*a*) The growth of weeds in a neglected garden and the development of bad habits in lazy pupils.

(*b*) Physics and mathematics

(*c*) Drawing and your specialty.

8. Explain meaning of "culture products of civilization."

9   Express agreement or disagreement with this excerpt: Correlation is not the teaching of two

things at the same time—that is not the meaning
at all, but it is using a fact or principle learned in
one study, to illuminate or demonstrate something
difficult of apprehension in another. Thus, grammar may be made to elucidate obscure or involved
sentences in the reading lesson; stories from history
brighten the details of geography, and the facts of
geography explain, as nothing else can, the movements of history; while the knowledge acquired in
arithmetic may be and should be used for quantitative work in every other subject, but particularly
in science, civics, and geography.—*Maxwell*.

CHAPTER IV

METHODS OF TEACHING

129. **Relation to science of education.**—Science requires exact classifications, but we cannot expect to find exactness until we have enough data for experimentation and verification. Some writers claim that education is entitled to be ranked as a science, while many others hold that education is still in a formative state. From its nature, education will always be in a formative state; but if any department or phase approaches scientific justification. methods of teaching must have that credit. It is a long era from Socrates to Herbart, but during all those years thinking men were formulating processes of teaching in accordance with the needs of the learners. The attempted adjustment of matter and mind was and is the vital consideration in method; it is what modern pedagogy is trying to accomplish by bringing teacher, pupil and subject-matter nearer the ideal condition described by the expression the meeting of the minds. We are still using too many names in our classification, but methods of teaching, as such, are not far from being effectual

It is not necessary to reproduce the two chapters,

METHODS OF TEACHING and GENERAL METHOD, pages 76 to 110 in *Methods in Education.* That treatment is authoritative, basal work. It is neither prudent nor logical for advanced students to try to interpret and apply high school or collegiate methods without first mastering those simple elements that constitute a clear concept. Apperception likewise demands the easy, natural order of development.

130. **Method and habit.**—The supreme value of method is the habit of mental activity acquired by the child. All processes and principles should be directed toward self-activity as a means of self-realization. Habits of definite, orderly, persistent work are the safeguard of the pupils when the pupils approach duties and tasks outside of the school environment   Methods are, therefore, casual in relation to efficiency in life.

131. **Monroe quoted.**—Method is the process of using this culture material so as to produce the desired development of the child; a development which will include the expansion of his own powers, the creation of control over them and the directions of them to the necessary, to the useful, and to helpful social activities. Method is the regulation of this process by the teacher. Method is the guidance of the child in his activities by the teacher so that he may incorporate into his own experience that portion of the experience of the race which, to those who have the direction of his education, seems valuable; that is, suitable for his stage of development and similar in complexity to his own

interests and activities The sole effort of the teacher should be directed toward the guidance of this process; his sole interest should be in the expanding consciousness of the child, in furnishing experiences appropriate to the power of the child and properly related to his interests and activities —*Text Book*, p. 757.

132. **Methods dependent upon mind.**—Methods of teaching depend, in a last analysis, upon the acts of mind involved in sense experience and thought. First impressions are prone to inadequacy and even incorrectness. A complete survey of the act of knowledge will show three steps in method; observation, deduction, induction —*Dictionary of Psychology.*

133. **Classification.**—Oral language is the natural means of communication; hence, there is the conversational method. Inquisitiveness finds expression in questions, and thus the question method signifies instinct and intelligence. Knowledge is not gained at a single bound; hence, the development method is both cause and effect. The varying needs of individuals required various stimuli to produce reactions, and thus the development method had to yield to different kinds of approach—inductive, heuristic, concrete. A single experience of joy, pain, fear or hunger led to a conclusion that became a race habit, and the deductive method lived as an infallible process for centuries. We might go on to justify each of a score of meth-

ods by instinctive laws, but further suggestion is
unnecessary. Better turn to the tendency to con-
solidate and eliminate, and, by doing so, arrive at
this simple classification:

> Analytic—synthetic
> Inductive—deductive
> Topical
> Socratic

134. **Topical method.**—The wide use of this arrangement of facts makes the topical method the
most popular one in high school work. As we have
said elsewhere, the advantages of the topical
method are convenience in assigning lessons, definite responsibility in recitation, and independence
of pupil in thought and expression. The disadvantage comes only from abuse in which facts are
disconnected and class stimulus is sacrificed to individual achievement.

It should be noted that the topical may or may
not be logical. Very little matter in school books
is arranged according to the rigid laws of logic.
The five formal steps of instruction are logical, and
outlines in grammar may be so; but daily work
in literature, composition and history is likely to be
arranged according to more flexible standards.

The use of the topical method should be advocated as a means of teaching pupils how to study.
The habit of observing things as they are expressed
by others, the habit of selecting essentials, the habit
of organizing the facts selected, the habit of studying the facts as arranged in outline form, the habit
of oral reproduction or written reproduction, and

finally the habit of relating this sectional outline with preceding and following sections,—all are habits that should be blended into one in school work. Compare with Earhart's *Teaching Children to Study* or McMurry's *How to Study* or Dewey's *How We Think*.

CHAPTER V

GENERAL METHOD

135. **Meaning.**—The operation of the human mind is such that it is possible to formulate one method that is valid for all human beings and all subject-matter.

136. **Basis.**—The justification of this claim was found in the analysis of apperception. Herbart considered apperception the one great process in learning; and out of his study of the process, came the conclusion that there is one effective method of presentation, namely, general method as embodied in the five formal steps of instruction.

137. **Ideal.**—The aim or ideal in education is the concept. Socrates thought so too. Both Socrates and Herbart advocated a formal procedure as a means of causing the mind to work rightly. With Herbart, the *process* was exalted; so again we turn to method for desirable habits of activity. Observe always how general method is related to the apperceptive process, concepts, and desirable habits.

138. **The steps.**—*Methods in Education*, page 100. Another explanation by DeGarmo follows: (1) *Preparation* This consists of a brief preliminary review of such acquired knowledge or experi-

ence as will best fit the child's mind for a rapid and interested appropriation of the new matter about to be presented. (2) *Presentation* of the new lesson. (3)*Association.* This stage provides for more complete apperception of the facts of the new lesson by associating them intimately with related facts already acquired. (4) *Generalization.* This stage gathers up the facts of the lesson in such a manner that their deeper inner significance may be grasped by the pupil. In many studies these generalizations appear in the form of definitions, rules, principles, laws, maxims, &c. (5) *Application.* By this stage is meant those drill and practical exercises which tend to fix knowledge in mind, and to secure a facile application of it to practical affairs. As may easily be seen, these stages are but an amplification of observation, deduction and induction, the three logical steps found in all experience and thinking.—In *Dictionary of Psychology.*

139. Method-whole.—This term has been used to designate the subject-matter suitable for teaching by the general method. In other words, any portion of matter that could be arranged for lessons so that the process of teaching went from the particular to the general and then back to the particular, was called a method-whole. The term is going out of use; lesson plan and lesson unity are substituted.

140. Generalization.—This step has been spoken of as the most important one in all education. Why? Think how many acts are involved as the apperceptive process transfers the thought from the particular notion to the general notion and thus puts the idea into the sphere of abstract knowledge. Think of the blending of the products observation, memory, imagination, reasoning and judgment; think of comparison, the laws of similarity and contiguity; think of abstraction, a process that distinguishes man from man by the degree of mental acuteness; and finally think of generalization, the climax of induction, the one distinctive intellectual act which lifts the human species far above all other forms of creation. Truly generalization is a wonderful summarizing process, and yet how many of us stop to consider that it is the one thing pupils are trying to accomplish?

141. Individual opinion.—In all the work in this chapter and in the succeeding chapters, students should recall and apply the substance of the preceding matter in this book. Add to this your own practical experience with pupils. While an acceptable viewpoint must be held, students should express themselves with a certain degree of independence as long as the expression is based upon experience that has produced satisfactory results. It is neither necessary nor desirable to try to get students to adapt themselves to one mould of opinion. Nor would it be possible to do so, if it were desirable

Section 142 contains an abstract from an article by Dr. Hervey, of the New York City Board of Examiners. In agreement with other educators, he expresses a liberal view. The abstract is taken from *New York Teachers' Monographs* for December, 1902.

During this year (1911) much has been written to discredit general method. It is probable that less attention will be directed to the formal steps, but still some of those steps must be retained as essential mental acts. Dr. Hervey's thought is worthy of analysis, even though general method may not remain a cherished inheritance.

142. **Dr. Hervey** quoted.—"The central problem of instruction considered as a formal process is the problem of making knowledge our own; the key to the solution is the nature of the mind itself; and that view of the mind which helps in this problem is the view which regards the mind as an arrangement for converting stimuli into reactions, for transmuting experience into knowledge and knowledge into life. Under this view there are three basic and guiding principles.

(*a*) "Our thinking and learning is practical. As we think we are learning to act. As we act we are learning to think. Thought without a deed is not even a complete thought. In other words we learn to do by doing. Further, we should teach nothing that is not of use; finally, under this principle it follows that the idea of use or application must always be present. The maxims, 'Turn to use,' 'Learn through doing,' are akin to the maxims, 'Present to sense,' 'Present a good model,' 'Teach objectively,' 'Evoke the will.' For when we act and when we turn to use we are willing and we are dealing with matters at first hand. We are getting *sensations* of acting, which sensations are the basal elements in our education.

(*b*) "No knowledge can lead to action and bear on life unless it appeals to the imagination. The abstract by itself cannot influence life. The road to the will is through the concrete (i. e., through presentations and representations) or through the abstract supported by the concrete. The conclusion is: 'When teaching that which involves mental imagery see that mental imagery is called up in the minds of those taught.'

(*c*) "Instruction must not stop after sensation and imagination. 'The end of instruction is the formation of general ideas' Sense and imagination alone are not sufficient to form the circle of thought which education should produce. The products of sensation or of imagination stand out as single acts and it is the purpose of instruction to have these single acts analyzed and then expressed in the form of a law, a maxim or other general statement. This law is a general concept or a general notion. The general concept holding together many particulars answers to a consistent and well-ordered course of action, in which means are adjusted to ends and other means are in reserve to meet emergencies. Unless individual notions be so organized, subordinated, concatenated, the action resulting will be scrappy, spasmodic, inappropriate, inconsistent, ineffectual and self-destructive. If these three laws are satisfied apperception will take care of itself."

Under these general laws it is believed that there

is a certain order of the mind in every complete act of instruction. This matter has been explained in section 138 in this chapter. Continuing in his article, Dr. Hervey emphasizes the point that the five steps need not come in the order in which they are mentioned, but they all should come somewhere in every complete act of instruction. He cautions teachers against making the preparation too long because he has observed that pupils' minds have wonderful powers of adjustment to a straightforward and even blunt approach. He thinks that preparation instead of standing alone at the beginning of the recitation occurs at each step in teaching; each step should prepare for the next. Good teaching from start to finish is steeped in preparation. Preparation is no more an antecedent of the first step than it is of the third; hence, preparation may involve the presentation, thought, or application or all of them; and second, that each of these involves preparation. There are an infinite number of preparations within each method-whole, and there should be infinite variety in the method of handling them. Nor is it necessary that comparison and generalization should hold rigidly to the order in which they are named, for we frequently ask children to think and afterwards to imagine.

Conclusion. "The human mind, (generally speaking) is not a blunderbuss. Yet from the directions for making lesson plans which I have known to be given to advanced classes by teachers of the formalist type, it would appear that teaching the mind is precisely analagous to loading a brass cannon. Swabbing, taking aim, loading with powder and shot, ramming home, setting off the fuse, all must come in a certain order not to be deviated from. Such a figure limps on both feet. In more senses than one it smacks of militarism. One who is appealed to by it belongs in a factory where things are made, or on the firing line where people are shot at, not in a school where minds grow and are fed.

"Therefore, the best way, in my judgment, to profit by the doctrine is not to think chiefly of steps, or of sequence, or of separateness, or of junctions at which one must change cars for the next step— the best teachers when at their best are, I trow, not thinking about the formal steps—but to think chiefly of the ideal end of instruction, as being that happy state of pupils' minds in which, for warmth and resource, there are abundant stores of concrete imagery, and, for economy and serviceableness, there is organization-pigeon-holes and tags, card catalogues and indexes, or if you will, generals, lieutenants, and privates, each knowing his duty and each on the qui vive to do it. The formal steps are, then, so many ideals which the teacher must attain before his work is done "

Examination Questions

143. It is a chief business of education to pass from distinctly perceived individual notions to clear general notions.—*Pestalozzi.*

(*a*) Explain what is meant by individual notions.
(*b*) By general notions. (*c*) Give an example of
passing from individual notions to general notions
(*d*) Describe briefly a mode of teaching which vio-
lates Pestalozzi's principle.

144. Certain methods or devices are sometimes
used by a teacher with great success for a time, after
which they are no longer effective Why is this?

145. "Verbal reproduction, intelligently connected with more objective work, must always play
a leading, and surely the leading part of education
* * * The great difficulty with abstractions is
to know just what meaning the pupil attaches to
the terms he uses. The words may sound all right,
but the meaning remains the child's own secret."—
James.

Describe, with illustrations, two ways by which
the teacher can find out whether the pupil attaches
(approximately) the true meaning to his "verbal
reproduction."

146.

(a) What is it to generalize?

(b) What is the use of generalizing?

(c) What are the chief obstacles to correct
generalizing?

(d) How, in your specialty may the power
to generalize be developed?

147. Show the psychological necessity of aim in
every lesson.

148. "Preparation, presentation and application
are necessary in every complete act of instruction."

What is educational significance of "complete act of instruction"?

149. References.

DeGarmo. *Essentials of Method.*
Gordy. *A Broader Elementary Education.*
Lange. *Apperception.*
McMurry. *Conduct of the Recitation.*
McMurry. *General Method.*

CHAPTER VI

PRINCIPLES OF EDUCATION

150. **Meaning of principles.**—This term is used under various significations in philosophy, but our purpose is to have it express a definite meaning in education. Webster says a principle is "a fundamental truth; a comprehensive law or doctrine, from which others are derived, or on which others are founded " A principle of education is a law that applies to the human mind whenever the normal human mind is exercised in the process of learning.

The principle of apperception alone can be interpreted broadly enough to include all other laws or principles as ordinarily discussed in books on education. Herbart's use of the term in this sense has already been spoken of as justifiable. But clearness in explanation seems to demand a classification including at least four principles of education, as follows:

The principle of attention.

The principle of interest.

The principle of apperception.

The principle of self-activity.

While the psychical processes in apperception include attention, interest and self-activity, it is obviously easier for young students to plan their

63

work and justify their teaching acts by citing the four principles. See page 41 in *Methods in Education.*

151.   **Meaning of maxim.**—A maxim of education is a law whose application is limited   Most of the maxims apply to elementary education. For instance, concrete to abstract is a maxim seldom observed in college instruction.

152.   **Distinction not observed.**—The distinction made here is not usually observed, but it is advisable, nevertheless, for students to hold to the statement that only universal laws can rightly be called principles. The limits of time do not permit students to make application of more than four principles of education in oral or written discussion; and the requirements of logical division would scarcely admit more than two headings, *self-activity* and *apperception* The safe rule is the requirement of the case. Take apperception alone, or two headings, or four headings, and see if the following so-called principles are more than maxims or axioms:

1   Reactions.
2   Motivation.
3   Visualization.
4   Motor activity
5.   One thing at a time.
6.   Multiple sense appeal
7   Learn to do by doing.
8   Processes before rules.
9.   Observation before reasoning
10. From the simple to the complex.
11   From the empirical to the rational.
12. From the concrete to the abstract.

13   From the particular to the general.

14.   Facts before definitions or principles.

15.   Self-activity is the source of knowledge.

16.   From the known to the related unknown.

17.   Never tell a child what he can find out for himself

18   Atttention on the part of the learner is the condition of acquiring knowledge

19.   The mind must gain through the senses its knowledge of everything external to itself.

20.   There is a natural order in which the powers of the mind should be exercised, and the corresponding kinds of knowledge taught.

21   The mind can exercise only a definite amount of energy at any one time. This amount varies with age, natural ability, and degree of development

Attention

153. **Attention defined.**—Focussed consciousness is attention.

Attention is the centering of the act of any faculty upon its object, by an impulse of the will.—Welch, *Psychology*, p. 5.

Consciousness occupying itself with an object is attention —Horne, *Psychological Principles of Education*, p. 314.

Attention is that act of the mind by which we bring into clear consciousness any subject or object before the mind.—Gordy, *New Psychology*, p 111.

Attention is concentrated consciousness   Attention is not a faculty of the mind, it is simply a concentration of consciousness upon some particular object, external or internal.

154. **Training attention.**—Some one has spoken of attention as the mind at work or beginning to work upon its object. It is the aim of education to habituate the child to acts of attention so that the acts shall become responsive to the child's need. The purpose is more than focussing consciousness intermittently; the purpose is the formation of serviceable habit. Here the question arises, Is attention a common or constant function of the mind, or is it a variable and specialized function? In other words, Is there a general power of attention, or is it a power resulting from many separate acts of attention? Modern pyschology favors the theory of many acts resulting in habit; i e., many attentions, many memories, etc.

A quotation from James is suggestive here, no matter what our psychological interpretation of attention may be. In the chapter on **The Stream of Consciousness** in his *Psychology*, he says: "Consciousness, then, does not appear to itself chopped up in bits Such words as chain or train do not describe it fitly as it presents itself in the first instance. It is nothing jointed; it flows. A river or stream are the metaphors by which it is most naturally described In talking of it hereafter, let us call it the stream of thought, of consciousness, or of subjective life."

155. **Kinds of attention.**—Involuntary, reflex, passive, spontaneous; voluntary, active; sensorial,

or attention to an idea; ideational, or attention to an idea. For general purposes, involuntary and voluntary are the two classes students should know. The work of education is to form the habit of voluntary attention.

Securing and retaining attention.

Elaborate the points given here in relation to securing and retaining attention.

1. Comfortable environment.

2. Personality of teacher; attractive appearance, inviting manner, persuasive voice.

3. Habit of expectancy in pupils in relation board, charts, presentation of lesson, drill and assignment.

4. Orderly, progressive questions; get pupil to ask himself questions.

5. Responsibility; pupils feel that the teacher has confidence in their willingness to contribute to success by being attentive.

156. Helpfulness of attention.—Attention aids the physical process by enabling the senses to make better observation; stronger nerve currents reach the brain, thus assuring intensity of impression. Attention aids the psychical process by holding the image until the mind makes the percept clear and distinct; later, attention helps in forming clear concepts. In physical or psychical processes, time is an element, and attention assures time enough for apprehension and retention. Thus attention is causally related to vividness of thought.

Interest

157. Interest defined.—Interest is psychologically both objective and subjective. Objectively, interest is attached to some person or thing, the latter being either abstract or concrete. Subjectively, interest is a moving power well expressed by the ordinary use of the word feeling. These definitions give acceptable interpretations.

1.   The feeling attached to an idea is interest.

2.   Interest is the name given to the pleasurable or painful feelings which are evoked by an object or an idea, and which give that object the power of arousing and holding the attention.—Dexter and Garlick, *Psychology*, p. 31

3.   Feeling, so far as it is taken out of its isolation and put into relation to objects of knowledge or ideals of action, is interest.—Dewey, *Psychology*, p. 276.

4.   A genuine interest is nothing but the feeling that accompanies this identification of the self through action with some object or idea.—De-Garmo, *Interest and Education*, p. 27.

5.   Herbartian doctrine of interest. "The doctrine that the interest naturally attaching to the ends for which pupils study should be awakened in the means (i. e. the studies) used for reaching them; and, conversely, that permanent interest in the ends should be fostered through the means."

158. Kinds of interest.—Native, acquired, individual and scientific.

Native interest is instinctive attention; sometimes called spontaneous interest.

Acquired interest is native interest transformed to suit needs by use in adaptation to environment. Education begets acquired interest

Interest possessed by one person in one thing, or by one person in several characteristic things of his own, is individual interest. The oneness of the interest is noticeable; it is particular rather than general.

Interest in a class or a group of things, persons, places, etc., having some common characteristic, is scientific interest It is general rather than particular.

Gordy says· Individual interest and scientific interest may be distinguished by illustrations. The distinctions may be made by illustrations from botany, zoology and psychology. The particular flower which grew from a seed and which you yourself have planted, which you have nursed and cared for from the beginning, botany cares nothing for. You may be a botanist, but as such you are interested only in the universal aspects and relations of plants. The same is true, of course, of all the sciences. Your dog that you have taught to know and love you, that barks with delight when you come, and looks at you so longingly when you go, is an object of interest to you, but not to the zoologist Zoology cares for him only as a type, queries whether creatures of his class can reason, studies the resemblances and differences between the class to which he belongs and other closely related classes. The same is true of psychology. Contrast the point of view of psychology with that of the mother toward her only child To the mother he is the centre of life and affection for whom she has lived and suffered, for whose sake she would willingly die. To the psychologist he is merely a specimen of the human race; all that makes him precious in his mother's eyes the psychologist cares nothing about —*Broader Elementary Education*, p. 188.

159. **Herbartian doctrine applied.**—To be interested in a thing is to be in love with it. This kind of feeling develops into *desire*, and desire into *will*. Instead of considering learning as an aim and interest a means, Herbart would make learning develop an interest that would last till the end of life. This kind of interest is called "direct interest" in opposition to "indirect interest" which pursues an object, not for its own sake but for some intellectual or material advantage "The more the indirect interest predominates," says Herbart, "the more it leads to one-sidedness if not egotism." The one-sided individual approaches egotism even if he himself does not notice it, for he relates everything to the narrow circle for which he lives and thinks

160. **Many-sided interest.**—This expression is Herbart's. Many-sidedness must be distinguished from exaggeration, dabbling in many things. It is many-sided but not manifold. The man who is interested in art one day, then turns abruptly away from it to pursue science, then devotes himself wholly to sport, etc, has not a many-sided but a sporadic interest which, at bottom, is merely another expression for one-sideness.

There is another kind of many-sided interest condemned by Herbart It is that interest which expends itself in certain directions to the neglect of other directions. For instance, a teacher may take an interest in every one of his pupils but, at the same time, have such an interest in certain ones that he really neglects the others. *Herbart's many-sided interest means balanced, proportionate or equilibrious interest. In common language it means harmonious development of powers*

Applying the idea of many-sidedness of interest to the school, he writes· "One cannot expect that all the different classes of interest will unfold themselves equally in every individual, but among a large number of pupils they must all be expected and the demanded many-sidedness will be all the better cultivated, the more even the single individual approaches a mental culture in which all those interests may stir with equal energy."— Lang, *Outlines of Herbart's Pedagogics*, p. 21.

161. **Circle of thought.**—The circle of thought for any pupil is the limit of personal interest of the pupil in the subject-matter of instruction, or in matters outside of the school It is distinctly the work of education to extend the circle of thought so that the pupil may become interested in as many lines of investigation as he is capable of carrying on without reaching the result known as smattering in education. The five-fold division of the course of study in our elementary schools illustrates a many-sided interest which should give every pupil the desired circle of thought to prepare him for

future efficiency. An application of extending the circle of thought. is found in Lang's *Educational Creeds*, page 150: "A boy spends his play hours in fishing, catching birds or butterflies; and he is in danger that his fine feeling, sympathetic heart will harden. Would punishment direct the content of his will to nobler pursuits? Would it thoroughly cure him? Certainly not. It would sooner increase the dangers. The thoughtful educator pursues a different course. He seeks to build up a new interest in the thought-circle of the boy. He calls his attention to the beauty of the flowers, explains to him their nature and various kinds, shows him how to raise plants and how to take care of them, how to press and dry them. The probabilities are that he will spend his recreation hours in cultivating plants, in botanizing, and in making a herbarium."

162. **Dewey's doctrine of interest.**—In *Interest as Related to Will*, Dr. John Dewey, of Columbia University, discredits the Hegelian theory of effort on the ground that the pupil's attention is divided during the performance of uninteresting tasks, the better part of the mental energy being permitted to wander to interesting considerations; and, secondly, the performance of such tasks being perfunctory, the will is not properly trained. Will-training is conditioned by the spirit or motive of the pupil. The Herbartian view of generating interest is likewise disapproved because it does not utilize self-expression. So Dr. Dewey concludes that *interest is self-expression.* His analysis shows

that an appeal to interest does not eliminate effort; and that effort does not lose its value in education simply because it is pleasurable.

163. Interest, effort, drudgery.—Much has been said and written about the respective values of the old and the new education in regard to making school work interesting for children. This is partly due to a misunderstanding of the various doctrines of interest; but still there is a diversity of opinion among those who clearly grasp the different views of interest, and so you should formulate a definite written opinion upon this topic. The following excerpts are suggestive.

164. Horne quoted.—"The true end of interest is not play, but work; not amusement, but solid achievement; not diversion, but productive occupation. Interest begins the process which effort ends. Interest is the path and effort the destination. Fortunate is he whose interest follows him within the gates of the city of his effort and takes up its abode with him there. Interest may be present in the final labor of effort, and is so in the final results of man's work, but it is necessary that the work be the fruitage of the interest. The essential thing is that the interest lead somewhere and be not mere pastime. Thus interest is the means to effort and effort is the end of interest.—*Principles*, p. 323.

165. James makes interest and effort compatible.—After admitting that most school work is repulsive to pupils, he says: "The repulsive processes of verbal memorizing, of discovering steps of mathematical identity, and the like, must borrow their

interest at first from purely external sources,
mainly from the personal interests with which success in mastering them is associated, such as gaining of rank, avoiding punishment, not being beaten
by a difficulty and the like Without such bor-
rowed interest, the child could not attend to them
at all But in these processes what becomes interesting enough to be attended to is not thereby attended to without effort Effort always has to
go on, derived interest, for the most part, not
awakening attention that is easy, however spontaneous it may now have to be called. The interest which the teacher, by his utmost skill, can lend
to the subject, proves over and over again to be
only an interest sufficient to let loose the effort.
The teacher, therefore, need never concern himself
about inventing occasions where effort must be
called into play. Let him still awaken whatever
sources of interest in the subject he can by stirring
up connections between it and the pupil's nature,
whether in the line of theoretic curiosity, of personal interest, or of pugnacious impulse The
laws of mind will then bring enough pulses of effort
into play to keep the pupil exercised in the direction of the subject There is, in fact, no greater
school of effort than the ready struggle to attend
to immediately repulsive or difficult objects of
thought which have grown to interest us through
their association as means, with some remote ideal
end.

The Herbartian doctrine of interest ought not,
therefore, in principle to be reproached with mak-

ing pedagogy soft If it do so, it is because it is
unintelligently carried on Do not, then, for the
mere sake of discipline, command attention from
your pupils in thundering tones Do not too often
beg it from them as a favor, nor claim it as a right,
nor try habitually to excite it by preaching the importance of the subject. Sometimes, indeed, you
must do these things, but, the more you have to do
them, the less skillful teacher you will show yourself to be Elicit interest comes from within, by
the warmth with which you care for the topic yourself, and by following the laws I have laid down.—
Talks, pp 109-110

166. **Roark approves Herbartian doctrine.**—
The most important service rendered by Herbart,
next to his showing the intrinsic economic value of
interest in securing attention for rapid and effective
work, was his insistence upon interest as desirable
in itself, as a pleasant, comforting, and sustaining
state of mind The best and highest application
of the doctrine sends students forth from any grade
alert to see and hear the best, eager to know, open
minded to the truth, full of noble aspirations.

Herbart showed how the emotional nature,
which had been for centuries condemned and suppressed in the schools, could be made the main-
spring of right action and a source of legitimate
joy. There is no conflict whatever between this
idea of interest and the idea of duty, or even of the
necessity of drudgery. The feeling of oughtness
is innate in the human being, and the performance
of duty gratifies this feeling and so prompts to the

further discharge of duty. So far from there being antagonism between drudgery and interest, it is interest that makes the performance of drudgery possible. Drudgery may be defined as work which is uninteresting in itself, but must be done in order to the attainment of some end that is desired. Interest carries the worker through the drudgery to the desired result, and hence the need that the teacher shall often direct the attention of the pupil to ultimate goals, fixing his interest upon them, and showing from biography, past and present, how faithful application to the present task will lead to the full satisfaction of his right ambitions. The function of the teacher is not to follow blindly the interests of the pupil, but to arouse in him interest in the work he ought to do. One of the highest pleasures comes through the consciousness of overcoming obstacles, of facing down a disagreeable thing, to reach something finally worth while.—*Economy in Education*, p. 215.

167. **How to secure attention.**

1. Teach pupils how to work: consciousness of power to accomplish something.

2. Sympathy, leadership, recognition of meritorious results.

3. Adaptation through proper grading and grouping: discouragement obviated.

4. Useful methods in teaching: graphic, varied; processes worthy of imitation when pupil is studying alone.

168. **Relation of attention and interest.**—Attention and interest are so closely related that

one cannot persist without the other. Which comes
first? Put your thought into practical ways of securing and retaining both and then answer the
question by interpreting results   Attention is an
attitude of mind and body growing out of and en-
forcing a feeling called interest.   Both attention
and interest are habits.

Apperception

169.   **Importance of apperception.**—The simplest
analysis of mental activity will reveal the importance of apperception in education   It is implied, of
course, that perception precedes apperception; but
after the first percept became a mental possession,
every subsequent act of getting a percept employed
apperception   Likewise in memory and all other
manifestations of mind. Without apperception, no
knowledge is possible, and without activity, no apperception is possible   Thus education itself is conditioned by the quality and the quantity of self-
activity in the apperceptive process.

170.   **Apperception defined.**—Mental assimilation, or the interpretation of new knowledge in the
light of that previously obtained, is apperception.

171.   Apperception is the process by which a
mass of presentations assimilate relatively new elements, the whole forming a system   The new material assimilated may be either given in sensation
or reproduced by the internal working of the
psychological mechanism, and attention, in the
broad sense of noticing an object, coincides in the

main, but not altogether, with the apperceptive process.

172. The process of attention in so far as it involves interaction between the presentation of the object attended to, on the one hand, and the total preceding conscious content, together with preformed mental dispositions on the other hand — *Dictionary of Philosophy and Psychology.*

173. Derivation of the word apperception.—The word "apperceive" is derived from *ad,* to, *percepere,* to grasp or to clasp   It literally signifies the grasping or clasping of one thing to another, a uniting, adhesive process.   But the Latin verb also means *to see* or *perceive·* so that taken figuratively apperceive means *to see or perceive one thing by way of another,* or the coalescence of a new idea with an old one by modification.—*Burk A Hinsdale*

174. Apperception is synthesis.—The term is largely used by educational writers to characterize the synthesis of new with old experiences.   New acquisitions of knowledge become significant only to the extent of the interpreting power of our former acquisitions.   This being the case, the apperceptive power of the mind is a constantly developing capacity as the child increases in years, knowledge and mental alertness.   Modern child-study emphasizes the fact that the subject-matter of instruction, together with the sequence of its topics, and the time of its presentation, should be covered by the child's power to apperceive   Furthermore, methods of teaching and of moral training should take their

cue from the same changeable power.—*DeGarmo in the Dictionary of Philosophy.*

175. **Processes in apperception.**—The Herbartian interpretation of this mental activity may be expressed in modified form, as follows:

1. A perception calls up older related ideas.

2 These older ideas, which we call apperceiving ideas, or apperceiving mass, come forward to meet the perception.

3. Assimilation follows, that is, the new and the older ideas mutually change each other so as to bring about similarity.

4. The two ideas (or masses of ideas) are blended in consciousness

5. The enlarged idea produced by assimilation takes its place in the circle of thought and becomes a new apperceiving basis for subsequent use.

176. **Gordy's analysis of apperception.**—We see also in what this activity consists It is a relating activity—in sensation, bringing characterless experiences into relations of likeness and difference, in perception, combining sensations into relations of space; in memory, combining the various elements of experience into relations of time; in conception, percepts into relations of likeness, in judgment, combining percepts and concepts into the various relations of reality apprehended by the mind. If, then, we adopt the name usually applied to this activity and call it apperception, we see that apperception is that combining activity of the mind that brings order and harmony into our mental life

by transforming the consciousness of related facts "into the consciousness of relations "

Apperception, then—of which, indeed, discrimination and assimilation are modes—is the most fundamental form of mental activity It makes sensations, and then, in the form of discrimination, separates those that are unlike and assimilates those that are alike; it discovers the space relations of sensation, transforms them into attributes of bodies, and then discriminates the objects so perceived that are unlike, and assimilates those that are alike; it discerns the time relations of mental facts, and transforms a succession of experiences into a consciousness of succession; it combines percepts into concepts, percepts and concepts into judgments, judgments into conclusions.—*New Psychology*, pp 352, 353.

177. **Apperception related to interest**—Three conditions are mentioned in getting the relation of apperception to interest If perceptions or sensations are quickly blended with the apperceiving ideas, there is facility of apperception *Facility* gives rise to a feeling of *delight* "This, in turn, awakens the *wish* to have the same mental activity repeated, and produces a *need* to continue the occupation with the object that caused delight Hence it is the *facility*, the *delight*, and the *need* which make the apperception to that which Herbart calls interest."

178. **The teacher's problem.**—These sections on apperception suggest a desirable scope of inquiry for students. The teacher's problem is not easily

stated in a sentence, since every teaching act requires adjustment to the needs of individual pupils In teaching pupils how to observe, does not the process become one of adapting the varying capacities to the object? The apprehension of details is nothing more than effectual apperception. In training the memory, we think of apprehension, retention, and reproduction Not one of these can be considered as a psychical process apart from apperception. What can be done with reasoning and judgment without going to apperception as fundamental? Comparison of ideas implies the holding of ideas in the mind while similarity and contrast enable the thinker to accept or reject. Thus the teacher's problem is to harmonize personality, matter and method in establishing relationships between the new and the old The maxim, *from the known to the related unknown*, has pertinent significance here.

Self-Activity

179. Self-activity is instinctive.—The axiomatic meaning of this word suggests at once the characteristic instinct of all normal children. It seems almost useless to ask students to deal with obscure definitions of this term, better look to the one large purpose of all educational agencies, namely, to organize the tendencies of activity. This organization requires interpretation, aims, process and results in both theory and practice.

180. Self-activity defined.—It is not easy to define self-activity, but every teacher knows that activity, physical and psychical, is a charateristic of childhood   If education means an adjustment to environment, it needs no argument to show that all activities should be directed toward the highest possible degree of useful efficiency.   Under such a view self-activity means self-realization   Other definitions follow:

Self-activity, as a principle in consciousness, means self-direction —*Horne*

Conscious effort in the evolution of possibilities is termed self-activity.—*Boyer*.

Self-activity is activity "that contains its primal impulse within itself", it is activity that is self-conscious, self-asserting, self-determined, self-expressing, and in the largest sense self-realizing. Self-activity is thus another name for the activity of spirit; and the problem of self-activity is seen to be one phase of the problem of spirit, how to maintain the primacy of spirit, how to nourish and promote the life of spirit.—*Hervey*

181.   Opportunities for activity.—It is a duty of the teacher to give the child every possible opportunity and incentive for expressing himself—in language, in gesture, in vocal music; in various forms of play; in constructive activity with pencil, brush, tools, or the hand

The child who learns at school to draw, to model, to paint, to sew, to cook, to make things in wood and iron, to sing, to speak and write effectively, to carry himself in a way that expresses his character, finds within himself a fund of resourcefulness, a degree of self-poise and efficiency, and a capacity for enjoying life, which passes the understanding of those who have not had such advantages.

It is error to suppose that creative activity is limited to the making of external products There is an element of such activity possible in every educative exercise, just as the lack of it is apparent in an ill-conducted class in manual training. The teacher should aim to evoke the highest possible degree of self-activity in every legitimate form, in every exercise.—*W. L. Hervey, in Teachers' Monographs*, October, 1901.

182. Thorndike on limitations of activity.—This principle should not be misunderstood It does not mean that pupils should be encouraged or permitted to enjoy unrestrained activity. It means mental, moral and physical activity under the direction of the teacher Such direction leads to proper habituation.

Least of all should anyone confuse self-activity with bodily activity, or take responses to mean only gross physical movements. The child who sits quietly absorbed in solving a problem is more active and more truly active than his neighbor in the next seat who is jumping up and down with glee at getting the answer The activity of thought indeed often involves the cessation of many bodily actions.—*Principles of Teaching*, p. 40.

183. Substitution applied.—The aim in successful teaching is to utilize instructive activity by directing it into habits of useful application It is no longer justifiable to ask children to sit still for long periods; nature never intended human beings to become fixed machines. An aim or ideal is always made prominent as a stimulus to the intellect; through the feelings or interest, children are given a desire to attain the established aim; and then the will encourages activity toward the accomplishment of the desired end. Thus activity along desirable lines becomes a unification of mental, moral and physical effort. The habit of directed activity takes the place of inhibited action under enforced silence.

Suggestive Topics

184. Give a simple definition of apperception

185. Explain clearly what is meant by the apperceiving group.

186. Show the relation of attention to apperception.

187. Discuss three probable causes of defective apperception   Give remedies

188. Show how these four principles of education are practically applied in teaching pupils how to care for the school grounds.

189. Mention ten additional opportunities, aside from text-book study, for the utilization of self-activity. (Think of cleaning blackboards and show its educational value here)

190. In celebrating Memorial Day, how could the four principles be made operative in securing a desirable concept? State specifically what concept you aim to make.

191. Is stillness during the study.hour incompatible with vigorous mental activity? Compare Thorndike's conclusion in section 182.

192.   Define self-activity.

193.   **References on apperception.**—The import-ance attached to this one unifying process is likely to make apperception the leading topic in future classifications of principles of teaching For this reason, several references are given.

DeGarmo. *Essentials of Method,* chapters II, III.

DeGarmo. *Herbart,* Part II, chapter VII.

Dexter and Garlick. *Psychology in the Schoolroom,* chapter XIII

Dewey *Psychology,* pp 85-90

Gordy. *New Psychology,* pp. 346-364.

Harris *Herbart and Pestalozzi Compared, Ed. Rev.,* May, 1893.

James. *Talks to Teachers, chapter* XIV

Lang. *Outline of Herbart's Pedagogics.*

Lange. *Apperception.*

McMurry. *Elements of General Method,* chapter VI.

O'Shea. *Education as Adjustment,* chapter XIII

Rooper. *A Pot of Green Feathers.*

Stout. *Analytic Psychology,* Vol II, chapter VIII.

Stout. *Manual of Psychology,* Book III, chapter I.

Thorndike *Principles of Teaching,* chapter IV.

Witmer. *Analytic Psychology,* chapter I.

CHAPTER VII

INSTINCT AND HABIT

194. Recent opinion.—Recent investigation has tended to put the consideration of instincts into a place of prominence among educational essentials. Instead of treating instincts as characteristics of the lower orders of animals alone, we regard instincts as human tendencies which are worthy of direction.

195. Instinct defined.—An instinct is a useful act without prevision of the end in view.—*Horne.*

2. Instincts are called *race habits*,—habits acquired through the lifetime of a species, or perhaps an order, instead of during the life of an individual.

3. An inherited reaction of the sensori-motor type, relatively complex and markely adaptive in character, and common to a group of individuals, is instinct.—*Dictionary of Philosophy.*

196. Human instincts.—Bolton gives a long list and then makes a helpful distinction. Two paragraphs are quoted.

Among the most readily apparent human instincts the following are typical: Sucking, biting, clasping with fingers or toes, carrying objects to the mouth in childhood, crying, smiling, protrusion

86

of the lips, frowning, gesturing, holding the head erect, sitting up, standing, creeping, walking, climbing, imitation, talking, emulation, rivalry, pugnacity, anger, resentment, sympathy, the hunting instinct, migration; a great many fears or phobias, as of high places, dark places, strange objects; acquisitiveness, constructiveness, play, curiosity, gregariousness, bashfulness, cleanliness, modesty, shame, love, parental feelings, home-making, jealousy, pity. The list might be made vastly longer. In fact, man is a great complex of tendencies to acting, feeling, and thinking in a great variety of directions. These impulses are all instincts. Should some one argue that such a phenomenon as speech is not instinctive, but a result of imitation, I would make the rejoinder: "Then why does not my dog learn to speak the same as my child?" They both have the opportunity of hearing and imitating. The very fact that my child learns to speak while my dog does not is evidence that my child possesses a potentiality which my dog does not possess. This tendency or impulse is an instinct. Why is it possible for the cat, carried miles away in a bag, to find its way back unerringly? Or why can the homing pigeons and the bee fly in "bee lines," while we human beings make such sorry mistakes concerning directions? Because the cat, the pigeon, and the bee have potentialities which we do not possess.

Any activities or tendencies to action which are unversally possessed by a race or species,—which do not have to be learned by the individuals, or which are learned by individuals with great readiness, may be considered as instincts.—*Principles of Education*, p 151

197. **Important instincts in education.**—It is advisable to select the most prominent instincts or native impulses for the purpose of considering each one in relation to daily teaching   A list follows·

Physical activity.	Ownership
Mental Activity.	Kindliness.
Imitation.	Love.
Curiosity	Selfishness.
Sociability.	Pugnacity.
Play.	Independence.
Constructiveness	Defiance.

198. **Thorndike quoted.**—The following instincts are of special importance in school education:—(1) Mental Activity,—the tendency to be thinking in some way or another, to avoid mental apathy (2) Curiosity,—a special aspect of the instinct of general mental activity, the tendency to provoke ideas, especially in the presence of new situations.   (3) Physical Activity,—The tendency to be doing something, to avoid bodily torpor.   (4) Manipulation,—a special aspect of the instinct of general activity; the tendency to handle objects, to move them, take them apart, reunite them, etc., etc   (5) Collecting   (6) Ownership.   (7) Sociability. (8) Emulation   (9) Kindliness.   (10) Pugnacity and Mastery.   (11) Independence and Defiance —*Principles*, p 24.

199. **Desirable or undesirable instincts.**— Writers differ in making classifications under these two kinds   Many educators are inclined to believe

that there are no bad instincts, but there are undesirable instincts. Selfishness is undesirable, not bad. Education must accept selfish promptings as an indication of latent power which can be directed to good ends by substitution. So, too, with pugnacity, independence and defiance.

200. Aim in treating instincts.—We have said before that modern education accepts instincts as human tendencies that are subject to training by education; that direction of impulses toward desirable activity is better than curbing by authority; and that the period of human infancy permits development from purely instinctive action to rational self-control. The aim in treating instincts is, therefore, to encourage activity by directing native impulses through habit to self-realization.

Laws for Training Instincts

201. Inhibition.—The use of this word in education means the withholding of a tendency or an act for the purpose of forming the habit of self-control. Inhibition is used largely in reference to undesirable tendencies, such as lying, cheating, stealing; but the term applies as well in helping nervous children gain confidence, in keeping conscientious pupils from over-work, or in bringing scrupulous children to a safe standard of right living. Inhibition applies whenever we help pupils to work toward a more desirable ideal. Why is this psychologically true?

202. Disuse.—Disuse is frequently classified as a kind of inhibition, but it is rather the effect of inhibition. In a physical organism, an unused organ is likely to become atrophied. The strength of a muscle varies according to use or exercise. The same is true of psychical life; repetition is a necessity for the retention of facts. The theory of disuse applied to instincts means simply that an unused instinct fades away. Apply to cheating on examinations

203. **Suggestion from Thorndike.**—Disuse is convenient and is an excellent method to employ when the harmful tendency is transitory, but it is never quite sure. Punishment is ineffective in the case of very strong instincts To be of service in any case, it must be so administered as to connect the discomfort closely with the harmful act. Substitution is in most cases by far the best method for the teacher's use Habits of care for pets are the best preventive of cruelty to animals; to divide a class into two groups and give marks to the groups instead of individuals—to substitute, that is, team emulation for individual emulation,— may be the best cure for selfish ambition and envy; for a restless class manual work is better than scolding —*Principles of Teaching,* p 23.

204. **Inhibition by substitution.**—It is clear that disuse cannot be made effective unless we supply a substitute to satisfy human activity. So the whole process of mental, physical and moral education is a continuous effort in establishing more desirable thoughts, language and deeds than children would experience without the aid of education

Here, as elsewhere, the word education includes all the agencies discussed in preceding chapters.

205. **Inhibition by repression.**—This kind of training does not utilize the law of self-activity. Corporal punishment illustrates inhibition by repression. The evil tendency of the child may be inhibited temporarily by fear or pain, but no desirable occupation or habit is assured after the sense of fear passes away. For a suitable remedy, go back to the law of subtitution

The application of this law of repression is a debatable matter. Should it never be used? Interpret the psychology of your own experience and then frame an opinion.

Theory Applied

206. **Pugnacity directed to good use.**—This quotation from James expresses the thought of the majority of experienced teachers.

Pride and pugnacity have often been considered unworthy passions to appeal to in the young. But in their more refined and noble forms they play a great part in the schoolroom and in education generally, being in some characters most potent spurs to effort. Pugnacity need not be thought of merely in the form of physical combativeness It can be taken in the sense of a general unwillingness to be beaten by any kind of difficulty. It is what makes us feel "stumped" and challenged by arduous achievements, and is essential to a spirited and enterprising character We have of late been hearing much of the philosophy of tenderness in education, "interest" must be assiduously awakened in everything, difficulties must be smoothed away. Soft pedagogics have taken the place of the old steep and rocky path to learning But from this lukewarm air the bracing oxygen of effort is left out It is nonsense to suppose that every step in education can be interesting. The fighting impulse must often be appealed to. Make the pupil feel ashamed of being scared by fractions, of being "downed" by the law of falling bodies, rouse his pugnacity and pride, and he will rush at the difficult places with a sort of inner wrath at himself that is one of his best moral faculties. A victory scored under such conditions becomes a turning-point and crisis of his character. It represents the high-water mark of his powers and serves thereafter as an ideal pattern for his self-imitation The teacher who never rouses this sort of pugnacious excitement in his pupils falls short of one of his best forms of usefulness.—*Talks to Teachers*, p 54.

207. **Horne on use of instincts.**—Children are naturally constructive? Then provide courses in manual training and domestic science Children are full of play? Then provide ample recesses and good games, and recognize play as a legitimate educator and not as a necessary waste of time. Children are acquisitive? Then provide shelves for natural history specimens, encourage collections of stamps, pictures, flowers, etc Children obey the group or gang impulse? Then let home and school unite in organizing proper bands and clubs. Children have a curiosity surpassing that of any other creature? Then answer patiently their ques-

tion "Why?" as far as they are able to comprehend, and suggest further related questions to engage and develop their interest. Children have primitive fears? Arouse them, not by hobgoblin stories, but make the unavoidable consequences of wrong-doing such as justly to excite their fear. Children so easily fly into a passion? When the fury is past, show the boy some wrong inflicted upon the innocent, and let his anger kindle as a flame to right it. Children are secretive? Agree with them to keep all evil reports about another. Children are so emulous of each other? Confront each one with his own weak past self to excel. They are envious of another's good fortune? Point to some man of good character as having the best treasure and secure hero-worship.—*Principles*, p. 268.

Habit

208. **Relation of habit to education.**—Long ago Rousseau said, "Education is certainly nothing but a formation of habits" This truth becomes more vivid when we stop to give reasons for the countless acts in the course of ten of fifteen years of school life. The whole period of infancy, whether covered by school education or not, is a time of habituation. Plasticity is conducive to development in accordance with environment. All the subsequent experiences modify the habits of infancy, but it is strictly true, in theory and practice, that the aim of all training is to form useful habits.

Habit Defined

209. Habit is that manner of doing or living which characterizes the individuality of man.—*Sabin.*

210. A fixed tendency to think, feel, or act in a particular way is a habit

211. Power or ability in man of doing anything when it has been acquired by frequent doing of the same thing, we call habit.—*Locke.*

212. Fundamental laws.—Three laws plainly stated are these ·

1. *Ideal* Ideal must be established to produce a motive. This appeals to the intellect, feelings and will

2. *Plasticity.* As nature guarantees this in youth, the educator's duty is to make use of it.

3. *Regular repetition.* The intensity of the impression can be made effectual only by regular repetition. Spasmodic effort cannot produce continuity of thinking.

213. Habits worth forming.—It has been said that industry, obedience and courtesy are three habits that assure success Larger lists are given in text-books on school management, but perhaps two opinions are enough:

By Dr. White—	*By Dr Maxwell*—
Regularity.	Neatness.
Punctuality.	Order
Neatness.	Punctuality
Accuracy.	Good Posture.

Silence.   Courtesy.
Industry.   Obedience, then respect.
Obedience.   Self-control.
                         Helpfulness to others.

214.   **Bagley on how to form habits.**—"Focaliza-
tion of consciousness upon the process to be auto-
matized, plus attentive repetition of this process,
permitting no exceptions until automatism results."

215.   **Horne on how to form habits.**—Quoted
from *Psychological Principles of Education*, p. 300.

"First, act on every opportunity.

"Second, make a strong start.

"Third, allow no exception.

"Fourth, for the bad habits substitute something
good.

"And, fifth, summoning all the man within, use
effort of will."

216.   **James on how to form habits.**

1.   "Launch ourselves with as strong and decided
an initiative as possible.

2.   "Never suffer one exception to accrue till the
new habit is securely rooted in your life.

3   "Seize the very first opportunity to act on
every resolution you make, and on every emotional
prompting you may experience in the direction of
the habit you aspire to gain.

4   "Keep the faculty of effort alive in you by a
little gratuitous exercise every day."

217.   **Rowe on how to form habits.**—As pre-
liminaries to habit-getting, (*a*) decide what habit is
to be formed, (*b*) determine the stimuli or situations evoking the reaction, (*c*) know definitely the

essentials of the best reaction. A teacher may fulfill these requirements automatically without consciousness of the fact. If they are not fulfilled,
whether consciously or not, only confusion results.

When fulfilled, the teacher is in position to
demonstrate the habit and teaching may begin, involving three additional factors—(*a*) working up a
strong initiative, (*b*) securing abundant and genuine practice (repetition in attention), (*c*) preventing
exceptions. The recommendations of James,
Thorndike, Horne, Bagley, Dumont, and Curtmann
either concur with these or offer suggestions for
the formation of habit which may be reconciled with
the four main divisions of the methodolgy of habit
stated above.—*Habit Formation*, p. 94.

Review Questions

218. Define instinct   Authority?

219. Define habit. Authority?

220. Make a list of eight instincts used in daily
school work.

221. Apply the law of substitution to laziness.
Tell specifically what you do in helping a lazy pupil
form a habit of industry.

222. "The great thing in all education is to
make our nervous system our ally instead of our
enemy"

Discuss this excerpt from James   If it is not
clear, read *Talks to Teachers*, p 66

223. Such school evils as carelessness, laziness,
tardiness, truancy, whispering, lying, cheating,
stealing, impudence and rebellion should be sup-

planted by the school virtues accuracy, industry, neatness, politeness, truthfulness, honesty, justice, punctuality, co-operation and obedience. The transition is a process of gradual habituation. Show the truth of this view.

224. Take opinion of Horne or James or Rowe and apply it to the teaching of a topic in high school work.

225. James says all instincts are impulses. What does he mean? Define impulsive action.

226. Show how you utilize the substance of this chapter in teaching pupils how to study. Choose a specified topic and then apply the laws of instincts and habits to (*a*) study period in school, (*b*) study during recitation period, (*c*) home study.

227. References on instinct.
ANGELL. *Psychology*, chapters XV, XVI.
BALDWIN. *Story of Mind*, chapter III.
JAMES. *Briefer Psychology*, chapter XXV.
JAMES. *Talks to Teachers*, chapters II, VIII.
MORGAN. *Habit and Instinct*, chapters II, VI, IX, X.
ROWE. *Habit Formation*, chapter V.
THORNDIKE. *Elements of Psychology*, pages 187-191.

228. **References on habit.**—Consult references in 227. Make a careful study of Rowe's *Habit Formation*.

CHAPTER VIII

DEFINITIONS IN PSYCHOLOGY

229. Scope of chapter.—These definitions are the ones covering the terms frequently used in the science of education. Other terms are used and other definitions are accepted, but this list is adequate for our purposes. A good text in psychology is needed by every student.

230. Abbreviations used in this chapter.—For convenience in consulting books which are easily secured in schools or libraries, the following abbreviations are used:

B. P. BALDWIN, *Psychology Applied to the Art of Teaching.*

D. DEXTER and GARLICK, *Psychology in the Schoolroom.*

Go. GORDY, *New Psychology.*

H. HALLECK, *Psychology and Psychic Culture.*

J. JAMES, *Talks to Teachers on Psychology, and to Students on Some of Life's Ideals.*

M. McLELLAN, *Applied Psychology.*

R. P. ROARK, *Psychology in Education.*

231. Consciousness.—Consciousness is the name given to all possible mental operations.—D., 2, 28; J., 15-20; H., 44-49; B. P., 31-33.

232. Mind.—Mind is a spiritual force that manifests itself in knowing, feeling, and willing.

For the general functions of mind, see B. P., 3-8, 35; D., 6, 7, 19-22, H , 49-52, J 22-28.

233. Phases of mind.—The three phases of mind are intellect or knowing, feeling or emotion, and willing or volition —D., 19, G , 163, 208; H., 51; R. P., 42, 67.

234. Knowing.—Knowing is the act of affirming the certainty of states of consciousness.

235. Feeling.—Feeling is a term that indicates pleasant or painful states of consciousness

236. Willing.—Willing is the act of the mind in making a choice of desires

237. ·Will.—The will is the power which operates in the mind in willing

238. Faculties.—A faculty is a mental power which acts upon objects, external or internal, and discriminates them from one another. We must not, however, think of the mind as composed of separate faculties The mind is a unit, but it can manifest itself in different ways; and for convenience we shall use the word faculties to indicate the different manifestations of power

239. Object, action, product of a faculty.—That on which the mind acts in the exercise of any faculty is termed the object of that faculty. I hear a peal of thunder; the sound so heard is the object of the faculty of hearing The action of this faculty is called listening, the product of such action on the object referred to is a notion or idea of the sound of thunder —*Welch, Teachers' Psychology*, p. 4.

240. Illustration of 239.—In teaching, the subject matter of instruction is the object; the principles of education are applied in the action; and the product is the ultimate purpose of all education.

241. Presentative faculties.—The three usually called presentative are sensation, perception and observation.

242. Representative faculty.—Memory is representative. It is taken up under these points:

Passive, rémembering; active, recollecting; the three steps—apprehension, retention, reproduction; the laws of association; mnemonics —B P , 96-99, 105-111, D , 110-116, 118-124, Go , 234-240; H., 101-112, J., 116-132, R. P , 79-90, 110.

243. Elaborative faculties.—The faculties involved in these thought processes are perception, imagination, conception, judgment and reasoning.—R P., 79, 109-114; D., 140-143, Go., 255-262; B. P , 102-104, 144; H., 150-158

244. Sensation.—A sensation is a state of consciousness resulting from nerve action.—*Halleck*, p. 59

A sensation is a simple mental state resulting from the stimulation or excitation of the outer or peripheral extremity of an incarrying or sensitive nerve —*Sully*. B. P., 18-30; D , 47-51 , H., 59-65.

245. Perception.—Perception is the general name of a faculty through whose action the mind gains knowledge, whether of things without or within ourselves Sense-perception is the faculty which supplies the mind with knowledge of external objects through the action of the senses of touch, sight and hearing In exposure to a storm I see, hear, and feel the driving rain. In this act of sense-perception the senses employed are those of touch, sight, and hearing. The object is the driving rain; the acts put forth are feeling, seeing, and hearing; and the product of these acts, while in progress, is a notion or *percept* of the rain. The percept in this case unites in itself the elements gained from feeling, seeing, and hearing If the object of my sense-perception had been a thing which was visible but not tangible, or audible, as a picture, a cloud, or a rainbow, the percept would have contained only the elements gained from the act of a sight.—*Welch*, p. 5

B P., 38-40; D , 57-61 , H., 67-76

246. Observation.—The special function of the senses is sensation, a responding to any external stimulus that affects nerve tissue. The corresponding function of the mind in referring these sensations to their external cause is perception. Sensation and perception taken together may be called observation.—R. P., 68.

B. P , 91; D , 82-84; Go , 227-228

247. Simple definition of observation.—Observation is the act of looking at a thing closely so as to take note of its several details and parts

248. Memory.—Memory is the faculty which unconsciously receives, retains, and restores, the products or ideas gained through the action of the other faculties.—*Welch*, p. 6.

D , 110-116, J., 116-132; H , 101-112; B P., 96-99, 105-111; Go., 234-240, R. P , 79-90, 110

249. **Imagination.**—The process of making images is imagination. An image is a revived percept.

250. **Conception.**—Conception is a mental process which results in a concept —D , 150.

251. **Concept.**—A concept is a re-presentation in our minds answering to a general name.—*Sully.*

252.—**Judgment.**—A judgment is an assertion of agreement or disagreement between two ideas.—D., 163

253. **Reasoning.**—Reasoning is the faculty that derives new truths or concepts from class concepts already known.—*Welch*, p 11.

254. **Attention, etc.**—For attention, interest, apperception and self-activity, see chapter VI

Divisions and Distinctions

255. **Percept and perception.**—A percept is a psychical product; perception is the process and it is largely physical A percept may be compared with a particular notion

256. **Concept and conception.**—Concept is the mental product; conception is the process A concept is known as general notion, notion, or idea.

257. **Particular notion.**—The knowledge gained about any individual thing is a particular notion Our first acquaintance with any individual object gives us a particular notion Percepts are individual notions gained through the senses; but inner observation may likewise produce a particular notion. DeGarmo says our knowledge starts with individual notions (*Esssentials of Method*, page 17), but others dispute this statement.

258. General notions.—The passing from particular to general by the process of generalization gives the general notion or concept. Common nouns usually express what the mind holds as a general notion

259. Abstraction.—The mental process of passing from concrete particulars to the idea expressed by laws, rules, definitions, or general truths, is abstraction. The mind actually draws away the essentials to be combined in the concept.

Abstraction: another meaning.—In learning how to study, the pupil avoids distractions by fixing his attention on the point to be mastered The act of drawing the mind away from non-essentials, or essentials that are diverting attention, is called abstraction. The derivation of the word suggests the meaning.

260. Concentration.—The act of fixing the attention on a desired object is concentration of mental power. Intensive study or any other form of mental application is known as concentration of mind. Note how many of these conceptions go back to the principles of education.

261. Suggestion.—Suggestion is the tendency of consciousness to believe in and act on any given idea.—Horne, *Principles*, p 284.

262. Order of developing faculties.—The natural order of development is perception, memory, imagination, conception, judgment and reasoning. But since the mind is a unit, the development of one implies the use of the others.

263. Habituation.—The series of acts in the

formation of habits is habituation.   Habit is a result, habituation is a process.

264.   Visualization.—The act of learning by seeing things as they are, is visualization.   Apply the
foregoing terms—suggestion, concentration, abstraction.

265.   Mind-wandering.—The tendency of mind
to go away from a present object of effort is called
mind-wandering.   Does it indicate less concentration of effort?   James says mind-wandering is not
always fatal to mental efficiency.   If one really *cares*
for a subject, the mind will return to it after wandering in other fields and will get more out of it
than another mind which works continuously but
less intensely.—(*Talks*, 114).

266.   Impulsive action.—See instinct.

267.   Reflex action.—Reflex action is the power
possessed by the spinal cord and medulla oblongata
of transforming afferent into efferent impulses
without the interposition of the brain.—*Dexter and
Garlick*, 15

268.   Reaction.—Reaction is response to stimulation.   See *Methods in Education*, p. 42.

269.   Ideo-motor action.—An action resulting
from an idea in consciousness is ideo-motor action.
In youth, impulsive action is frequent; in adult life,
inhibition operates more frequently.

270.   Motivation.—Motivation is literally the
moving or influencing a person by an ideal   In
school work, motivation has reference to the purposive effort stimulated or caused by an effectual
appeal to intellect, feelings and will.

CHAPTER IX.

ADOLESCENCE

The Boy and the Girl in the High School

By Professor J. M. TYLER, of Amherst College

---

271. The girl at sixteen has attained her full height and practically her adult weight, though this increases in both sexes far into adult life. The boy has somewhat still to gain in both respects. The lungs of the boy have increased markedly in capacity at fourteen and again at sixteen In the girl the increase is far less marked or regular. The heart, which was small at eight and eleven, has gained greatly in capacity during puberty. In a few years its increase may amount to one hundred or even more cubic centimeters, a gain of more than sixty per cent. The same increase takes place in the girl in a shorter space of time, sometimes in two years. The arteries have expanded much less than the heart. Hence the blood pressure is high

272. The brain has attained practically its full size and weight, though it may increase very slowly until after the thirtieth year The sensory and motor centers are fully matured. The higher mental areas are in a stage when a good amount of exercise will do them no harm. The logical powers are increasing fast The boy often argues from the love of debate quite as much as from the desire to attain the truth. Mortality, though rising, is still low. Morbidity ought to be low at this time, but sometimes or ·often it remains high in the girl. In both sexes there is a rise and maximum of sickness at the close of growth, which healthy training and conditions should greatly mitigate

273. Vigorous physical exercise can now do only good. The muscles are ready for their final training Mere play is not enough; gymnastics are needed It is a time when athletics are exceedingly useful, but they can easily be made too severe. The great increase of the heart has been accompanied by the addition of much new tissue, hence it is weak and easily strained Century runs with the bicycle and long halves at football should be carefully avoided The boy is still far from the toughness and endurance of later years, when the tissues have gradually matured and hardened Every commander of an army recognizes the high rate of sickness and death among young recruits on hard campaigns, especially in unhealthy or severe climates Now the hard bed with light coverings in the cool room and cold bath will help the hardening process in the healthy boy. The danger of overpressure from study is probably not so great in the high school as in the lower grades.

The greater danger is of too much and too intense social life, and the accompanying excitement, late hours, and loss of sleep. Whether the last years of the high school course are too crowded for the best mental development of our boys and girls is a question which must be answered by experienced observers.

274. The attainment of full growth and of large muscular power, the large heart and lungs, the well oxygenated hot blood driven at high pressure, the activity of young vitality of all the tissues and systems, give buoyancy and courage, a sense of power and longing for complete freedom, and revolt against control. A new world opens before him, as fresh and fair as on the morning of creation. The glory of life, the joy of mere living dawns upon him. He sees parents and teachers plodding in a humdrum round. He is sure that they cannot understand him, and that they know very little of the glories of life and of the world. He will gird his loins, go whither he will and learn all about it He must taste of every experience, and is willing to meet both joy and sorrow with "frolic welcome." He has not yet been saddened by experience, or dis-illusioned by disappointment and failure. He would eat of the tree of knowledge of good and evil though it should cost him paradise Nature is now loosing her leading strings. He is set free to complete his individual development and to forge his own character. We cannot stop him if we would, we should not if we could. In old times the adolescent ran away to sea, now we send him

away from home to school or college. Authority
has only a superficial hold upon him, tradition far
less. But the influences of home training, which
have rooted themselves deep in his subconscious
life, are still very powerful He has not yet gained
self-knowledge or self-control Much of the child
still lingers in him Impulses well up from every
change in his physical constitution or condition,
and he is entirely unprepared to meet them He
hardly knows his real strength, much less his weakness. He is very loyal to his associates, as is
shown by his group games, his class and society
feeling, and his school or college spirit To understand him under certain conditions you must have
studied the psychology of the mob; instability
often seems to be his most marked characteristic.

275. He is a mixture of contradictions, an
enigma to us and to himself. He might well say,
"My name is legion, for we are many " In the
ferment of his young life all that is trifling and
worthless comes to the surface; the strong and
sweet lie beneath the froth. We may very easily
do him injustice If we cannot understand him
and sympathize with him, we should very carefully
leave him to nature. Let us not forget that forty
years ago the Union was saved by an army of boys.

276. He has hardly clearer conceptions of the
meaning and value of time than a child. He cannot
play a waiting game If the sun shines to-day it
will always remain cloudless. If the maid of his
adoration has frowned upon him, she will never
smile again. He lives on the Delectable Mountains

or in the depths of the Valley of Humiliation, more frequently in the latter region than you suspect. He betrays all his conceit, his humiliation over blunders, failures and sins he feels, but keeps to himself. Such is, or soon will be, the boy or girl intrusted to the care of the teachers in the high school.

277. Let us try to look a little deeper. The boy has a great heart, is loyal to his friends, devoted to his leader. He is often generous to a fault. Deal honestly and "squarely" with him and you may apply curb or spur as you will His system of morality may be crude and strange, but he is usually true to it. We must trust him, even if he does now and then disappoint us.

278. Tides of religious thought and tendency have swept through his soul, corresponding to the periods of acceleration of his physical growth. The first may have come at twelve or even earlier, and is often weak and apparently lacking in permanent results. A second follows at fourteen, stronger but largely emotional The wave at sixteen affects feeling, intellect and will Or religious growth and development may be gradual and steady. The importance of all these changes cannot be over-estimated; the mental metamorphosis at adolescence is just as profound as the physical at puberty. All things are becoming new We must expect it to be a time of instability, of surprises, and of contradictions. Perhaps you see only the beginnings of this process; but the preparation and beginning largely determine the final results,

279. It is the period of promise in the life of the boy and girl It is often our privilege to catch a glimpse of these promises, to "see them afar off" before they are even suspected by parent or friend. They "see visions and dream dreams." There are endless possibilities in these dim and far off visions. Mr. Phillips said that the power which hurled slavery from its seat was young men dreaming dreams by patriots' graves The all-important question now is: Can the promise be made good and the visions realized? The dream has more substance and value than all the rules of prosody, propositions of mathematics, or facts of anatomy. . . . . .

280. This power of arousing the higher divine life immanent in every human soul is the essential character of the great teachers, leaders and prophets of all time. Its seat is in the depths of personality; it defies alike analysis and resistance. It leaps from soul to soul as if by contagion Heroism evoked by hero worship is the central thought of all history from Gideon and his three hundred to Sheridan at Winchester changing a mob into an army of heroes

Virtue streams out from strong character, but it is exceedingly infectious, and good is more infectious than evil. If we amount to anything, we are sources of infection, whether we will or not.

281. Hence courses, methods, training and instruction, all together, are of less importance than

the personality of the teacher.   Kipling's Sergeant Whatisname

> "   .   .   .   drilled a black man white, he
>   made a mummy fight,
>   He will still continue Sergeant Whatis-
>   name.
>   Private, Corporal, Color-Sergeant, and In-
>   structor—
>   But the everlasting miracle's the same "

. The everlasting miracle is the final secret and essence of education, and the use of school and college is to bring pupil and teacher near enough together so that it will work itself   If we teachers are good for anything, we are putting into our pupils something better than our life-blood.

282.   We must be healthy in mind and body, or we cannot be strong, and strength streams only from the strong.   We must be sympathetic, for sympathy is the cable along which the magnetic power of personality flows.   With children we must be a child, a boy with the boys.   Otherwise the bond is broken, or never formed

283.   We must be patient, hopeful and courageous.   Else the child or man will not trust us, and will have none of us   Evidently we must catch this personality from someone else, and can transmit only what we have received.   Hence a teacher who does not believe with all her heart in the communion of saints will never be a real educator, however much Greek or history she may know, or however firm and wise her discipline.   We must live in constant association with the noblest souls.   We

can easily find them among our immediate neigh-
bors if we search aright; if not, we must seek
them in literature and history   We must gain ad-
mittance to what Heine has called "the apostolic
succession of great souls, the only people who
understand anything in the world."   And we must
change into their image.   We are called to the very
grandest of all professions.   We cannot be sufficiently proud of our calling, or sufficiently
humbled by the smallness of our attainments   We
make the Massachusetts of the twentieth century.
We are doing something far grander.   We work
for the development of the race.   We mould it into
conformity with what is deepest and most permanent in environment.   Hence all the powers of
nature are with us.   We cast in our efforts with the
irresistible tide of events as it sweeps toward a
better age   Let us "be strong and of very good
courage "—In *Education*, April, 1906.

Adolescence Discussed

284   The discussion in this section is the work
of one of our students

The period of adolescence marks the transformation of boys and girls into men and women.   There
is a marked step in the development of the physical
nature.   The girls generally attain their growth by
the age of sixteen, and the boys by the age of
eighteen.   There is also a marked development of
the sexes during this period.

The youth and maiden are not content with the

companionship in games and plays—there is a desire to express and exchange ideas, thoughts, feelings and sentiments

During this period the tendency of heredity to assert itself is strong, there is a liking for solitude, a feeling of irresponsibility, a lack of motor control, and a greater feeling of self-consciousness.

The rapid building up of the physical nature (rapid growth, increased sensibility of the skin and sense organs, the increased supply of blood) brings in an element of excitement and great physical vigor, and at the same time there is a fluctuation of activity and dullness. The dullness follows as a result of too great an expenditure of the extra vigor and energy

There is likewise a constant change of interest and fads. The ambitions and ideals undergo a constant readjustment; and it is the beginning of soul stirrings.

The period of adolescence is certainly one which needs to be surrounded by much care, wholesome interest and tactful watchings and suggestions. Because of the suddenness of many awakenings and changes, their diversity and shifting character, there is great danger that harm rather than good may follow in their steps. They need to be helped in their weaknesses; to be allowed fads which will outrun themselves if judiciously handled; to be given healthy outlets for their superfluous physical energy and changing interests; and to be led out of their embarrassing self-consciousness. Physical and mental fatigue and strain are far more injurious to girls than to boys during this period. Boys are likely to suffer from the result of too little rather than from too much activity at this period

The character of studies of this period should help to tide over this important period of life successfully. If the studies are not characterized by vigor, irresponsibility will increase; the additional energy will spend itself in unnecessary and useless physical sources and there will be a lack of balance, their moral development is in a critical stage and vigor is needed   To meet the demands of this period aright and pass through it unscathed the will power stands severe tests—therefore the need of "strong exercise of will" in the studies.

Energetic emotion is a natural outlet for some of the extra energy; but the emotion must be energetic or it may degenerate into sentimental lines Dreaming, love of solitude and wandering, formations of ideals, desire for companionship of opposite sex—these and others of their kind are characteristics which can easily be made a source of strength or weakness.

My own view of the characteristics of pupils during this period has been embodied in the above statements and explanations; the same is partly true of my view concerning the work to be done in it during this period

I might add that the best of manly and womanly ideals should be presented to counteract any weak or false ones; that the foolishness and silliness and smartness of this age should be tactfully discouraged with firmness; that the painful self-consciousness should be met with gentleness and consideration, and not with ridicule or harshness; that the teacher must be on guard against over-fatigue for the girls and lack of activity for the boys

Quotation from Authority

285. **Definition.**—Adolescence is the period in the development of the individual introductory to the attainment of maturity. Legally, it is from 12 in girls and 14 in boys to 21; physiologically, to about 25 for boys and 21 for girls.

286. **Physiological characteristics.**—The term is usually, but not exclusively, confined to human developmental stages. It is customary to distinguish the periods of infancy, childhood, puberity, adolescence, the adult state, and senescence; a distinction between the early and the later periods of adolescence seems also desirable. The more distinctive characteristics of adolescence are of a physiological nature related in great part to the unfoldment of sexual functions; but the accompanying secondary psychological tendencies are hardly less characteristic and important. The appearance of the beard, the change in voice, the assumption of the adult form, the more pronounced differentiation of sex characteristics, the final consolidation of the bones, the appearance of latent propensities, the change of features to show new characters, the prominence of hereditary influences, as well as other less objective and more subtle changes, serve to distinguish adolescence.

287. **Psychological traits.**—The psychological traits of adolescence are prominent, but their variability and complexity render an adequate description difficult In thought and feeling, as well as in appearance, the boy becomes specifically masculine and the girl feminine. There is in both a fundamental change and expansion of the emotional life The mind is filled with hopes and ideals, dreamy longings and fervid passions. Ethical, religious, and intellectual motives become more cogent; conscientiousness and seriousness inspire action Great emotional fluctuations occur; periods of enthusiastic energy and spasmodic attempts at high achievement giving place at times to languor and depression, to doubt, dissatisfaction, and morbid rumination It is a period of violent affections for the opposite sex, of intense friendships, of pledges and vows. It is a period when home surroundings begin to seem narrow, and the desire to wander, to do and dare, seizes the adolescent enthusiast. It is the period of adventure, of romance and poetry and artistic sensibility In its later stages it may usher in the period of doubt and speculation, of the desire to reform existing evils, and the ambition to accomplish great things Many deeds and movements of historical importance found their origin in the impulses and strivings of adolescents, while the description of this period in their own career or in that of others has offered an inviting field for the biographer and the novelist. The storm and stress periods of Goethe and John Stuart Mill, of Tolstoi and Marie Bashkirtseff, no less

than the masterly delineations of George Eliot's Gwendolin Harleth and Maggie Tulliver, form a valuable and suggestive contribution to the psychology of adolescence. The period has been recognized by primitive peoples, and in past civilizations by special rites and cults. In its educational as well as psychological aspect the study of adolescence is of great importance, the utilizations of the enthusiasm and good impulses and the avoidance of the dangers and the excesses of this period form a part of the duty of the educator, the physician and the parent, to which renewed attention is being directed—*Dictionary of Philosophy and Psychology.*

Adolescence Outlined

288. Summary.—This outline is intended as a useful summary of essential considerations in preceding and subsequent sections in this chapter Elaborate the suggested points in Sections 289 to 292 inclusive

289. Psychology of adolescence.
    1   Predominance of emotions Enthusiasm, joy, hate, etc.
    2. Introspection Extremes to be avoided.
    3. Higher cognitive powers developing
    4. Masculine and feminine types of mind
    5. Manners.
290. Morbidity of adolescence.
    1. Instability due to rapid development

of tissue. Biological proof.

2.   Danger in this unstable period.

3.   Greatest changes in reproductive, nervous, circulatory, and digestive systems.

291.   Disorders and diseases under 3 of 290.

1   Highly organized nerve tissue. Adapted activity, nourishment, rest.
(a) Neurasthenia and nervous prostration among pupils and teachers.
(b) St Vitus's dance and hysteria
(c) Melancholia.
(d) Hereditary diseases

2.   Anaemia, especially among girls.

3.   Dyspepsia and constipation

4   Disorders in reproductive systems. Necessity of prudent instruction of boys and girls. It is a false modesty that makes teachers overlook such private advice to pupils .

292.   Corollaries or deductions.

1.   Environment must be adapted to pupil rather than vice versa.

2.   Physical health is a predominant consideration.

3   Pupils need direction and inspiration rather than ponderous knowledge

4   School management is a vital consideration—discipline, studies, home lessons, study periods, recesses, food, clothing, and sympathy must be adjusted to the needs of the adolescents.

293. Write your opinion on this quotation: "Coeducation after the twelfth year is a mistake: better results for the race can be obtained by different systems adapted to each."

294. References.

Burnham. *Study of Adolescence*, in Pedagogical Seminary, I., 174

Butler. *Scope and Functions of Secondary Education*, in Educational Review, XVI., 19.

Christopher. *Growth and Development at Puberty*, in Transactions American Pediatric Society for 1901.

Clarke. *Sex in Education*

Ellis. *Man and Woman.*

Hall. *Adolescence*

Lancaster *Psychology and Pedagogy of Adolescence*, in Pedagogical Seminary, V , 61

New York Teachers' Monographs, October, 1901, p 63.

Warner. *Study of Children.*

CHAPTER X

MEANING OF TERMS

295. Specific viewpoints.—This chapter is intended especially for students who are preparing for examinations. Liberal scholarship implies breadth of view, but any examination for teachers' licenses is likely to require a specific expression of opinion. Such opinions must conform to an accepted standard of thought, no matter how strong one's own opinion may be. The aim of this chapter is, therefore, to help students focus their thinking on certain topics that are not clearly defined in educational literature.

Teaching Defined

296. By Joseph Baldwin.—Teaching is the art of promoting human growth. The efficient teacher understands the growing pupil and understands the subject taught. He completely adapts matter and method and leads learners to put forth their best efforts in the best ways.

297. By Edward Brooks.—The term *teaching* is a little more comprehensive that the word *instruction*. An instructor, strictly speaking, is one

120

who furnishes the mind with knowledge; a teacher
is one who furnishes the mind with knowledge, and
at the same time aims to give mental culture

298. **By Hathaway.**—Teaching is guiding the
pupil in those exercises which performed by himself,
will best develop his powers

299. **By Hinsdale.**—Teaching is bringing knowledge into due relation with the mind.

300. **By Hoose.**—Teaching is consciously ad-
justing objects and acts to the proper faculties and
capacities of the learner.

301. **By Laurie.**—Teaching is simply helping
the mind to perform its function of knowing and
growing.

Instructing Defined

302. **By Brooks.**—Instruction is the furnishing
of the mind with knowledge. It is the process of
developing knowledge in the mind of another The
term is derived from *in*, into, and *struo*, I build,
meaning I build into. To instruct the mind is thus
to furnish it with knowledge, to build up knowledge
in the mind.

303. **By Compayre.**—The principal means employed in intellectual education is instruction. There
is, in fact, no other way to develop the faculties
than by exercising them Now, intellectual exercise is study, and teaching is causing a pupil to
study

304. **By Roark.**—Instruction is directly giving
information—knowledge of facts, new ideas, and

words—to the pupil. It should be done only for the purpose of stimulating the desire for more knowledge, and of furnishing material that the pupil cannot economically get for himself.

Training Defined

305. By Sully...The systematic procedure of the teacher is implied in the word training. It means the continuous or periodic exercise of the faculty, with the definite purpose of strengthening it and advancing its growth.

Discipline Defined

306. Process and result.—As a process discipline is the exercise of an organ for the purpose of making it function more readily; as a result discipline is the power of performing economically and efficiently any work the organ would not have done so well without training. Recall formal discipline as a training that aimed to produce power to meet any emergency in life.

307. By DeGarmo.—Discipline is systematic training through education.

308. A quotation.—"Discipline is the result of training and study. In physical culture it gives a man control of his muscles, so that they are obedient to his will. In mental culture it gives him control of his intellectual powers, so that he is able under all circumstances to do the best work possible. In moral training discipline gives a man such control of himself bodily and mentally that he can resist temptation, discern good from evil. and make the best choice."

Study Defined

309. **By E. E. White.**—Study is the attentive application of the mind to an object or subject for the purpose of acquiring a knowledge of it. Study involves persistent attention, and continued or prolonged holding of the mind to the knowing of an object by acts of the will.

310. **By McMurry.**—These two definitions are taken from *How to Study*.

From Chapter II. "The term study as here used has largely the meaning given to it in ordinary speech. Yet it is not entirely the same; the term signifies a purposive and systematic, and therefore a more limited, kind of work than much that goes under that name."

From Chapter III: "True or logical study is not aimless mental activity or a passive reception of ideas only for the sake of having them. It is the vigorous application of the mind to a subject for the satisfaction of a felt need. Instead of being aimless, every portion of effort put forth is an organic step toward the accomplishment of a specific purpose; instead of being passive, it requires the reaction of the self upon the ideas presented, until they are supplemented, organized, and tentatively judged, so that they are held well in memory. The study of a subject has not reached its end until the guiding purpose has been accomplished and the knowledge has been so assimilated that it has been used in a normal way and has become experience."

311.   **By Earhart.**—Students should read *Teaching Children to Study*. This definition is on page 5.

"Studying in its highest sense is the process of assimilating knowledge, of reorganizing experience."

Learning Defined

312.   **Like apperception.**—Learning is apperceiving Mastery implies good apperception; and, as we have seen, thorough apperception includes all that the mind can do.

313.   **Examination question and answer.**—
(*a*) *Explain this rule of Jacotot's. "The pupil must learn some one thing and connect everything else with it." (b) What is properly meant by "learning" a lesson in geography or history? By "learning" a tune? By "learning" a stanza of poetry? By "learning" to be punctual?*

(a) There is no such thing as an isolated fact or idea. It must be associated with something else. Correlation of subjects, which received a considerable amount of attention, was a branch of this rule The "Compromise of 1850" means little to the pupil if he is not acquainted with the history of our country from the first appearance of the slavery question to the admission of California into the union.

(b) A lesson is learned in geography of history when a pupil, in his own language, is able to give the facts in their right relations. A tune is learned when a pupil or class is able to give it with ease and expression It may be with or without the copy A stanza of poetry is learned when the exact words of the author can be given without aid. Learning to be punctual means a repetition of the effort until it becomes a habit, when it is accomplished with ease

314. **Terms distinguished.**—Teachers are not necessarily educators Anything educates the child that helps to mould its character, or that stimulates its self-control Fire educates in an imperative manner, but it does not teach. The authority of the parent educates his child, while the child may be taught nothing in regard to the nature or source of authority. A teacher's personal influence may educate a school in ways of virtue, while he has taught them nothing about the nature of virtue Teaching regards the purely intellectual capacities of man. Education refers to all the capabilities of mind The intellect is taught by a person, and educated by persons and things The will is educated by any power. Teaching sets the subject-matter, trusting the mind to accept the truth ; educating may exert a power without giving any reason or instruction. Teachers should be educators. Parents are educators—they may also be teachers. Good teaching and good educating put the mind of him who is taught or educated, into a frame which acknowledges and accepts testimony and authority from whatever source they spring. That teaching or educating is pernicious which leaves the mind

of the learner in a state of undue skepticism towards testimony and authority.—*Hoose*.

315 (a). **To inform.**—To inform is applicable to matters of general interest; we may inform ourselves or others on everything which is a subject of inquiry or curiosity; and the information serves either to amuse or to improve the mind, to instruct is applicable to matters of serious concern, or that which is practically useful; it serves to set us right in the path of life. A parent instructs his child in the course of study he should pursue, a good child profits by the instruction of a good parent to make him wiser and better for the time to come; to teach respects matters of art and science; the learner depends upon the teacher for the formation of his mind, and the establishment of his principles. Every one ought to be properly informed before he pretends to give an opinion; the young and inexperienced must be instructed before they can act, the ignorant must be taught, in order to guard them against error. Truth and sincerity are all that is necessary for an informant; general experience and a perfect knowledge of the subject in question are requisite for the instructor; fundamental knowledge is requisite for the teacher.—*Crabb*.

Topics for Mastery

316. Sensations.
    1. Quality affected subjectively and objectively.
       a. Visual.

b. Auditory or audile
c. Olfactory.
d. Taste.
e Touch or tactile.
f. General · temperature, motor, common sense.
2. Intensity.
3. Vividness.

317. Perception.
1. Necessity of healthy bodies.
2. Attention to stimuli.
3. Apperception.
4. Expression

318. Memory.
1. Psychological stages
a. Apprehension.
b. Retention.
c. Reproduction.
2 Fixing impressions.
a. Receptive attitude of mind.
b. Regular repetition.
c. Physical fitness
3. Laws of association
a. Contiguity.
b. Similarity.
4. Kinds of memory.
a. Verbal
b Logical.

319. Imagination.
1. Reproductive.
2. Constructive.

320. Conception.
    1. Particular notion
    2 General notion.
    3. Generalization.
    4. Indistinct concepts caused by indistinct percepts, defective observation, poor abstraction, loose language, lack of time for assimilation, weak memory.
    5. Distinct concepts from concrete examples, wide induction, definite characteristics.

321. Judgment
    1. Relation between two ideas.
    2. Comparison
    3. Decision.
    4. Intuitive judgments
    5. Deliberative judgments.

322. Reasoning.
    1. Induction.
    2. Deduction.
    3 Analogy.

323 to 353. Logic.

Logic	Categorical argument
Syllogism	Hypothetical argument
Proposition	Disjunctive argument
Term	Dilemma
Definition	Fallacy
Division	Induction
Inference	Observation
Immediate inference	Explanation
Mediate inference	Method of agreement
Enthymeme	Method of difference

Argument
Hypothesis

Method of concomitant
variations

Method of residues

Rules of the syllogism
Rules of the logical definition
The law of identity
The law of contradiction
The law of the excluded middle
The validity of deduction
Rationalism, empiricism, reasoning, judgment.

CHAPTER XI.

SPECIAL PROBLEMS IN EDUCATION

Fatigue

353. **Explanation of fatigue.**—Prolonged exercise of any set of cells in the body results in fatigue. The cells become drained of their nutriment, exhausted, and so act with difficulty, if at all. The readiness with which fatigue of any part will be produced depends inversely both upon the development of the part and upon the state of general health. Since the nutriment of each cell comes from the blood, and since the amount of nutriment stored up in any cell will depend upon its size, a well-developed muscle in a healthy, ruddy boy can undergo exercise much longer before becoming fatigued than a poorly developed muscle in a pale, sickly boy; and the same is true in the case of brain activity.

354. **Effects of fatigue.**—The effects of fatigue, moreover, are noted not only in the part which has been exercised. A day of hard lessons produces a tired feeling all over the body, not simply in the head. This is because the nerve cells, by their activity, produce waste products, which are gathered up by the blood. These are irritating and affect the whole body, being carried to every part of the

blood. When during repose these products are got rid of, being burned up by oxidation and eliminated through the skin and other excretory organs, the tired feeling disappears. During the period of rest, moreover, the cells recuperate and reload themselves with nourishment from the blood, becoming again plump and ready for activity. Fatigue which can be readily dissipated by a night's rest is spoken of as normal fatigue, or as healthy tire. But if there persists a tired feeling in the morning after a good night's sleep, the fatigue is more than normal

355. **School work and fatigue.**—The amount of study or muscular exercise which produces simply normal fatigue in a healthy child may produce abnormal fatigue in a child who is physically below par; and if this amount of work is continued the child must have a nervous collapse, or nervous prostration. Children that are the offspring of alcoholic or neurotic parents, those that are anaemic, those that have defects of sight or hearing, those that are growing very rapidly, and especially young girls who are just entering the period of adolescence, are very susceptible to nervous collapse from overwork. Overpressure in schools is most apt to show itself in springtime, after the long winter, when the children have had little outdoor exercise. During this period of the year, moreover, increase in height is more rapid; this always causes great strain on the bloodmaking organs, and so predisposes to anaemia and hence to nervous exhaustion Mouth breathers and those children who have adenoid growths in the throat are also more liable

than others to anaemia and abnormal fatigue.

356. **Signs of fatigue.**—Awaking unrefreshed in the morning is one of the early signs of abnormal fatigue. Other signs are inability to concentrate the attention, loss of memory, irritability. If in a more advanced stage, there is morbid introspection and worry, perhaps hypochondria; next, there may be restlessness, diminished sensitiveness, and finally loss of ability to feel tired. Fortunately, the latter symptoms seldom occur in children. One result of over-fatigue is shown by the twitching movements of St. Vitus's dance. When any of the above signs appear, over-pressure in school is one of the elements to be thought of as a cause, and the child should be at once relieved of part or all of its school tasks. In writing on this subject Dr. Caille has said: "The days of brutally whipping children have gone. We are now refined and whip their brains to death." Children that are convalescent from an illness should be specially guarded against returning to school too soon, as they may develop defects of vision, as well as the general signs of abnormal fatigue.—Adapted from Article by Dr. LaFetra in *New York Times.*

357. **Meaning of fatigue.**—Fatigue is produced by a chemical process. Muscular action increases the oxygen absorbed and produces additional carbon dioxide. One of the principal substances produced by fatigue of muscle or nerve is lactic acid. There is a change not only in the size and microscopic appearance of the cell, but in histological appearance. It may be easily demonstrated that the

toxins formed in the blood by exercise are important, if not the principal causes of fatigue.—Bolton,
Principles of Education, 261.

358.   Use of the word fatigue.—The word fatigue is used in two senses. First, to denote the
feeling of weariness, second, the nervous exhaustion that results from functional activity of the
nerve cells. The former is a psychological fact, the
latter a physical fact.—Burnham, of Clark University, Worcester, Mass

359.   Some causes of fatigue.—

1.   Hereditary weakness.
2.   Vitiated air in homes and schools.
3.   Order of studies not adapted.
4.   Fear due to exactions of authority

360.   Questions answered.

1. *What is the explanation of the physical fact of
fatigue?*

The physiological explanation of fatigue is found
in the fact that in all nervous tissue there is a part
which is really living while other parts are coming
into life and still others are dying or dead   So by
fatigue is meant a condition where the constructive
or building-up process does not offset the destructive or breaking-down process involved in the expenditure of energy   It is probable, too, that weariness results when the waste products are not carried
away sufficiently by the circulation.

2 *Mention two deductions from physical and psychological fatigue?*

In both mental and physical activity there are
marked changes in the nerve tissue and every such

change is accompanied by waste. The real problem
becomes, therefore, a question of how to do a maximum of work with a minimum expenditure of energy. This in turn involves the determination of
suitable periods of work and rest under the psychological law of change, and it involves also a conservation of energy through proper habits of study.
Under this view, how to study becomes of para-
mount importance.

3. *What methods of measuring fatigue have been
tested?*

The first method is that of testing fatigue by
physical measurements before and after the period
of mental work. This is done by the Ergograph,
an instrument devised by Mosso, for measuring the
work done by a group of muscles. This method is
unreliable, as other causes than fatigue may vary
the results. Lack of interest by the pupil at different times of the day will cause a change in the
recording of the results. Then there is some painful experience in operating the Ergograph and this
would act as an inhibition upon effort.—See
O'Shea's *Dynamic Factors in Education*, page 181.

The second method is that of observation by noting the variations in mental work done during a
period of definite assigned work. "This method of
investigation was made by Sikorsky twenty years
ago by the dictation method and he found from
twenty to thirty per cent more errors after the
school work than in the morning; by Burgerstein
using simple arithmetical work for a test, the result
being a marked increase in the quantity but a de-

crease in the quality of the work during the course
of a single hour."

4. *Mention some of the characteristic symptoms of
fatigue?*

Restlessness, lack of power of co-ordination,
showing itself in the dropping of pencils and the
like, in slips of speech, and perhaps in uncertainty
in the use of the limbs, twitching movements, de-
creased sensibility, especially of sight and hearing,
flushing, unusual color of ears; and among the
mental symptoms, irritability, loss of memory for
common things, loss of curiosity and the power of
attention, disturbance of speech, etc.—Burnham in
Article on Fatigue, *New York Teachers' Monographs*,
October, 1901.

5 "The child, weary of the school task, turns
to what he likes and all evidence of fatigue disappears."

Explain this dictum according to the psychological view

This change is the psychological law of the rela-
tivity of feeling   The strong feeling of intense interest drives the relatively weak feeling out of consciousness until perhaps the latter becomes so great
that it reasserts itself and interest in turn lags, but
throughout the whole process the physical fact of
fatigue may have persisted

361. **Suggestive exercises.**

1. Make a list of the ways in which fatigue is
manifested by people whom you know. Make out
a list of the ways in which you think people in general and pupils in particular waste their energies.

2. Do persons who enjoy their work ordinarily

suffer from nervous prostration? Compare them in this respect with persons who regard their work as a drudgery, and then discuss this principle as it relates to school work.

3. "Yawning is a characteristic accompaniment of both temporary and permanent fatigue. The yawning is produced by anaemia of the brain. When one is temporarily fatigued, bored, or in a poorly ventilated room, the blood becomes stagnant in the small veins of the body. Those who suffer from cerebral anaemia yawn continually. The yawning, like stretching the arms, or massage, restores the equilibrium of the circulation."—(Bolton, 266).

How should yawning in school be interpreted (a) in relation to the teacher, (b) in relation to the pupil? What remedies do you suggest?

4. In this connection discuss the plan adopted in some cities of beginning school at 8.45 a. m. and going without intermission until 1 p. m. when school closes for the day.

5. Express your opinion upon these suggestions relating to elementary and secondary school work:

(a) Shortening the number of hours of work in the primary grades, especially for children who are easily fatigued.

(b) Adapting the length of each period of study or recitation to the age and physical fitness of the pupils.

(c) Granting a recess period for exercises in the open air, if possible.

(d) Alternating of difficult and easy studies and

also placing such difficult subjects as mathematics
in the morning, while manual training, gymnastics,
etc., may be put in the afternoon.

(c) Rational child study, so that management
of the school may satisfy the needs of individual
pupils.

Commercial Education

362. **The need of trained men.**—The development of commercial education is but one of the
striking instances of efforts now being made to
adapt education to actual community needs. Those
in charge of the secondary education have been
rather slow to realize that the old-time course of
study for high schools planned especially as a preparation for college was failing to attract or to hold
great numbers for whom preparation for vocations
is of immediate and pressing importance. In spite
of the fact that an almost insignificant proportion
of high school pupils seek admission to college, the
influence of the latter institutions in determining
the course of study for the lower school has been
all powerful, and the program neglected to those
subjects, however useful they might be, which did
not count specifically for college preparation. But
all that is changing. The secondary school is fast
coming to assume an independent position with its
own problems to solve in its own way, and these
problems concern themselves no longer chiefly with
the occasional student looking to a higher institution, but to the great numbers who must immediately take their place among the wage earners. Not

the least important among those problems is, in a commercial age and a commercial country, how best to prepare the youth to render intelligent and valuable service in the world of trade.

The marvelous inventions of recent decades, multiplying productive power, as they do, manyfold, and bringing the whole civilized world into wonderfully close intercommunication, enormously intensify division of labor, which involves and implies exchange and distribution, processes which are distinctly commercial. And with the vast increase in the extent of the exchange and distribution, there has come an increasing complexity in their management. Trade has long since ceased to be simple barter. Its rules and processes can no longer be picked up by the fairly intelligent in a few weeks. In its higher phases it puts to test the keenest minds, and in its ordinary phases it affords ample opportunity for the exercise of more than ordinary gifts.

If the secondary school is to render the best service to society, it must adapt its instruction to the needs of the time. If the activities of a community are chiefly or largely commercial, then provision should be made in the course of study for an educational preparation for these activities, and the preparation should not be merely general. It should include so-called "practical" studies. Those who have contended that education should look only to the cultivation of general power, and this acquisition of general knowledge, and should ignore everything designed to be immediately and directly useful, have argued ably, but they have not won their case. The unrest in secondary education noted by Commissioner Sadler in the very conservative German atmosphere owes its origin to the feeling that the training of the school should be more practical, and the same unrest is to be noted in every advanced community. Everywhere we note the loosening hold of the classical studies and the gradual exhaltation of the purely modern curriculum —*Principal J. J. Sheppard*, New York High School of Commerce, at N E. A , St. Louis

Manual Training High Schools

363. The manual training high school is peculiarly an American institution. England has higher technical schools, and the countries of continental Europe have many trade schools; but none of these perform the function of the American manual training school, which is in no sense a trade school but a special adaptation of education to our latest civilization. Although the nature of the human mind is essentially the same to-day as at the beginning of historic time, the education of the human mind has ever been compelled to change and adapt itself to the changing needs and experiences of human life. A liberal education, according to the ancient Persian standard, consisted of acquiring the ability to ride a horse, to shoot straight and to speak the truth Only one of these accomplishments is now deemed essential to education. The old classical form of education has held its place and has dom-

inated all education down to the latter part of the
last century on the fallacious theory that the education that was good enough for the best of men
300 years ago is good enough for all men now.
The error of that theory is too obvious to require
demonstration Indeed the fact that a system of
education is a hundred years old is now presump-
tive evidence of its unfitness for present conditions

From the old classical secondary schools there
have developed and for some time will probably
persist three general types of modern high schools,
namely, the literary, the commercial, and the technical or manual training. These are the natural
product of our changed industrial and social life.
A hundred years ago we were a nation of farmers,
producers of raw materials. Now we are a nation
of manufacturers and traders, and the army that
we have to fear is not the army of any nation
equipped with guns, but a German army of skilled
workmen, with tools in their hands, commanded
by captains of industry who have been educated in
the matchless Prussian schools. No artificial protection of our markets will permanently avail to
guard our industries against the invasion of that
army. Our only abiding protection must be found
in the training of our own workmen and in the education of our industrial and commercial leaders
Germany is years and years ahead of us in the special education of its workingmen. Berlin alone has
twenty-eight trade schools of various kinds.

The schools to which we must look for holding
our place in the industrial world are the technical,

or mechanic arts, or manual training schools, as
they are variously called; and these must not degenerate into mere trade schools. They must furnish academic training equal in quantity and of as
high quality as that furnished by the classical or
literary schools. They must require downright
hard book-work while teaching the elements of
many trades. These schools must prepare boys
for college and for all courses in college except
Greek. They must prepare for professional schools;
they must prepare for learning trades; they must
furnish the culture of a general education plus the
training of a technical education; and finally, they
must prepare young men for leadership in industrial
affairs. For these ends the academic studies of the
manual training school must be taken up somewhat
differently than in the ordinary high school. Mathematics and science must be taught with emphasis
upon the applications of these subjects to industrial
processes. It is asserted by enthusiastic advocates
of manual training that boys who are educated in
their schools accomplish very nearly as much in
academic studies as the boys in classical schools,
besides learning the rudiments of many trades
That they do this may be explained partly by the
fact that the work of the bench and the lathe comes
as a welcome relief from constant book-work partly
by the time saved from gymnasium exercises of
which boys in manual training schools do not require so much as boys engaged in sedentary work
only; but chiefly by the interest and enthusiasm
and spirit of work which pervades the manual

training schools Boys in these schools work harder and are able to work harder than boys in the ordinary schools and this spirit of work is noticeable in the boys who go on to the higher technical schools as contrasted with those who go to the academic courses in college. The university spirit of achievement and conquest pervades the technical schools.

The high schools are the poor man's opportunity to give his children a liberalizing education, and as such they are the educational hope of democracy. In view of the keen industrial and commercial competition of the times, these schools must be established and supported at public expense for social and economic reasons.—*Dean Ballıett*, School of Pedagogy, New York University.

Ideals in Military Education

364. **Loss in time, effort, results.**—"Enormous waste of time, great perversion of effort and correspondingly weak and inadequate results" were among the criticisms directed against the schools and colleges of to-day by Col C W Larned of the United States Military Academy, in the course of an address at Cooper Union, February 7, 1907. He said in part:

"The individualistic idea in education has led to a more or less chaotic state of things, not only in the medley of subjects offered for selection, but in the method of their teaching and the degree of application of the student in a 'go-as-you-please' sys-

tem   After desultory attendance at the various institutions for teaching from books the average
graduate drops it all and begins the serious work of
gaining money, or fame, or office. The student is
left as an undergraduate to do as he pleases, and is
taught to act in after life upon the same principle,
operating in and with the elaborate machinery by
which modern commercialism works.

"The long apprenticeship to learning has not of
necessity given the young man an improved body,
more skilled faculties, better habits of living, more
self-control, a knowledge of the duties of citizenship, a high respect for the rights of others, refined
moral perception, a knowledge of his own physical
constitution and its care, or of the duties and responsibilities of a parent. Strange it is that, although under training for years and years of his
impressionable youth, he should reach the fulness
of manhood and citizenship without discipline of
body, without trained respect for law, without
knowledge of his social obligations to his neighbor, or of the greater history of man in the struggle
of the masses for light and life and a fair share in
the bounty of God's providence In a majority of
cases he has not even acquired what culture pro-
fesses to give him—disciplined powers of thought.

"The military school trains for character and for
the state. It systematically develops the body and
it trains the mind along a consistent line for the
double purpose of clear thinking and effective practical work. It trains the character to discipline of
action, habits of subordination to lawful authority,

strict personal accountability for word and act, truth-telling, integrity and fidelity to trust, simplicity of life, courage.

"To-day higher education seems as a rule to concern itself no whit about anything but intellectual development or its technical applications, and its processes are mainly for culture or gain. Whatever influence is exerted upon moral, social, disciplinary, or physical development is incidental, sporadic, and feeble. Character is the essential meaning, in the last analysis, of every attempt I have seen to define education; and yet the practical mechanism by which education generally operates appears to me an exceedingly poor device to secure its development in its highest conception.

"What West Point does for its cadets is precisely this: It takes its youth at the critical period of growth; it isolates them completely for nearly four years from the atmosphere of commercialism; it provides absorbing employment for both mental and physical activities; it surrounds them with exacting responsibilities, high standards, and uncompromising traditions of honor and integrity, and it demands a rigid accountability for every moment of their time and every voluntary action. It offers them the inducement of an honorable career and sufficient competence as a reward of success, and it has imperative authority for the enforcement of its conditions and restraints.

"Unlike other institutions of higher education, West Point cannot be indifferent to the general performance of its students. It exacts of every individual rigid conformity to its standard, and its minimum standard is proficiency in every branch of study taught in its curriculum."

Opinion from Brown University

365. Pupils deficient in power to think.—President William H. P. Faunce, of Brown University, was one of the speakers under the auspices of the Department of Public Lectures of the Board of Education, 1907. Defend or disprove what he says about thought, judgment and expression.

"The young people of to-day, as compared with those of fifty years ago, are chiefly deficient in power of sustained attention and original thinking. They can not, or at least, they usually do not, think as clearly, as patiently, and as cogently as did their fathers. They do not as quickly distinguish the irrelevant from the pertinent, the kernel from the husk, as the men of the last generation. They have an amazing fund of information; they are wide readers of bright, ephemeral literature; they have tasted every fruit on the great tree of knowldge; they know a thousand interesting scraps; they are more versatile and ingenius and attractive than any other of the recent generations. But they are quickly led astray by sophistry, and easily led to surrender conviction when it conflicts with interest.

"Part of this is due to the universal reaction from the former drill and persistent iteration of the earlier teaching. In some schools the pendulum has swung so far that the clock has almost stopped.

To banish struggle as essentially evil is not only un-pedagogical but immoral. Gifts and games are good for little children, but the question still remains whether the boy can fall down stairs without crying, and tell the truth when it hurts him, and master a difficulty without promise of sugar, and face the little but real battles of his own intellectual and moral life without running away.

"A further object to set before our pupils should be greater power of self-expression through language. Many of our children have a poverty-stricken vocabulary, and rejoice in it. The remedy for poor modes of speech is not to be found in endless drill in grammar or markings with blue pencil, but in association with those who already know how to write and speak their mother tongue. Good English like good manners, is learned by association with those who have it

"Above all, the aim should be to develop the power to estimate mental and moral values. Many of the men who have been exposed as fraudulent in great transactions recently were not at all deficient in the three R's, they were deficient in appreciation of moral values. We need to paint the thing as we see it, and we need to see the thing as it is."

Secret Fraternities in High Schools

366. **Unsettled question.**—Express your opinion upon this topic. Defend either affirmative or negative, or discuss both points of view. Following is the consensus of opinion of principals in this country:

(1) That they are unnecessary for high school pupils living at home; (2) that whatever good might be claimed for college fraternities could not apply to boys of high-school age; (3) that public schools should be democratic and free from caste and organized snobbery; (4) that these fraternities among children do have a tendency to set up social exclusiveness and caste in the schools; (5) that they are a source of discord among the pupils, (6) that they become factional in their characteristics, and that loyalty to the fraternity generally breeds disloyalty to everything else; (7) that they dissipate the energies of the pupils and interfere with their studies; (8) that they are selfish and narrow in their aims and methods; that the conduct of the pupils should be open and above board, and there is no legitimate want or need in child nature which calls for secret or dark-lantern proceedings, and (10) that whatever of a social nature which it is necessary to encourage in school can be done through other and better forms of society which can be under the supervision and control of the principal. The best remedy for them seems to be to deprive the members of participation in all school affairs outside of the classroom —*G. B Morrison*, N. E. A , 1904

367. **Assignment.**—Read one of these references for the purpose of understanding fatigue as a cause or an effect of existing conditions in school life:

BOLTON *Principles of Education*, 260-302.

KIRKPATRICK. *Fundamentals of Child Study*, 321-333.

O'SHEA. *Dynamic Factors in Education*, 188-209,

CHAPTER XII

SCHOOL ADMINISTRATION

368. **Purpose of this chapter.**—The science of education implies continuity from the kindergarten through the university. It is the purpose of this chapter to treat the relationships which produce the desired continuity, but completeness of presentation of school administration is not attempted

In any good school system, the work of external organization is attended to by persons above the rank of the teaching force. This arrangement leaves the teacher to devote most of his energies to his own classes and the school in which he is teaching Thus out of his own experience he can estimate the pupils' progress, measure his own worth, and adjust himself and his work to the requirements of the system as a whole. After giving all due credit to the thought of others, the judgment of experienced teachers should be the one large factor in making an opinion for examination purposes or practical daily work. The various phases of management invite the translation of experience into expressed opinion

Principles in Management

369. **A reference.**—It is always advisable in facing a variety of opinions to select a few points and

148

organize them for a basis of discussion. Three pertinent principles are quoted on page 50 of McEvoy's *Methods in Education.* The study of the two chapters on METHODS IN SCHOOL ECONOMY and METHODS IN SCHOOL MANAGEMENT, pages 45 to 76 in that book, is recommended to all who believe that the principles of procedure in elementary education are valid in high schools and colleges.

Qualifications of Teachers

370. **How to estimate a teacher.**—Here, again, we meet a problem that is still in the realm of individual opinion. For verification of this statement, compare the plans for rating teachers in normal schools, training classes, text books on school management, and reports of school superintendents. A critical examination of the practice in New York City brings us at once to the point of acceptance, rejection or modification. Rejection requires an acceptable reason, modification must be justified by approved experience or authority; and, under any attitude, the final opinion should be one that contributes a wholesome view to the conception of this topic.

371. **Dr. Maxwell's address.**—On June 4, 1902, City Superintendent Maxwell delivered an address before the principals and other supervising officers in New York City. His subject was HOW TO ESTIMATE A TEACHER'S VALUE. He made a minute analysis of the kind of teacher which the Board of Superintendents wished to develop as the type of the

New York system. The address follows:

"I was especially requested to call this meeting by two prominent associations of principals in order that a clear idea of the new requirements in the rating of teachers might be obtained. The Board of Superintendents desires you to rate teachers under these heads: Teaching ability, scholarship, effort, personality, and control of class. Beside these details you are to give a general estimate. Those teachers deemed by you fit and meritorious in the sense that these words are understood in determining an increase of salary or in the renewal of a license should be marked 'A' or 'B', all others 'C' or 'D'. The majority, possibly a large majority, of the teachers will not reach 'A'. This is a mark that should be reserved for teachers of conspicuous ability.

"To define more closely the expressions used in detailing the teacher's value, 'teaching ability' is no doubt made up of many things, but we may pay especial attention to some very important ones. First, I would mention ability to impart knowledge, or as it has been termed, power of exposition. It is one thing to have an idea but a quite different thing to impart it. On the other hand, some teachers impart too much and leave the pupils little to do in the way of speaking and writing. Talking too much is a common fault of teachers.

"Another evidence of teaching power is the ability to interest pupils in subjects taught so that deep and lasting impressions may be made. Without the emotional force of interest the most accurate teaching fails to become part of the pupil's makeup.

"Another important sign of good teaching is the ability to train the pupils to good intellectual and moral habits. This is only another way of saying that the good teacher is a trainer and former of character. It is not of much account if a teacher teaches unless the learned develops an ability and a habit of learning. He should get especially a power of thinking, that is, of seeing relations of things, their likeness and difference, and so forth He should be able to reason. This should be seen to result in increased power of expression, statement in clear language and also in ability to do.

"It may be well, also, to mention some signs of poor teaching ability, things that would prevent a teacher from attaining a meritorious rating One is the requirement that recitations be in the exact language of the text-book—mere parrot work. Another is too much concert answering All concert work may not be bad, but most of it is. Another one is the neglect of the pupils' observing and inventing powers, as in drawing, where the poor teacher will tell too much and plan too much, destroying the pupil's individuality. Questioning is a valuable indication of a teacher's standing; we should observe whether the questions are well thought out and whether they are well distributed so as to keep all the class thinking and alert. A deplorable element of poor teaching is the neglect to employ object illustration in nature study and in every place where it is a fitting adjunct to the best understanding of the subject. Object teaching and illustration by diagrams is especially needed in arithmetic.

"A serious defect is waste of time. It may be the teacher's time or the pupil's, such as the dictation of examples in arithmetic or the slow and painful copying of paragraphs from the board.

"I will repeat, then, these are important considerations to note in rating teaching ability: Exposition or imparting interest, effect on intellectual and moral habits, parrot teaching, concert work, talking too much, telling too much, questioning, object teaching, waste of time.

"In rating for scholarship the principal should expect the teacher to have a good working knowledge of the subject she teaches. Her preparation for her daily lessons should also enter into her rating. Failure to prepare specifically for the work of the day is a conspicuous lack in the scholarship expected of a teacher. Dr. Arnold studied the lessons for his most elementary classes, for he said he wished the boys to drink from a full stream. It is possible for a lazy teacher to waste a great deal of the children's time and to bring a school into ill repute, as was the case of a teacher in one of our schools the other day teaching that there were three kinds of soil—dry soil, moist soil and wet soil. We expect our teachers to keep abreast of current events and to enhance the interest of everything taught whenever it may be related to matters of present or recent interest. A superintendent tells me of a class that has been studying the West

Indies as set forth in the geography, but the teacher told him that they had made no mention nor taken any notice of the astounding disturbances in Martinique, which have excited the sympathetic interest of the whole world.

"In rating a teacher's effort you should recognize her activity in school work and her efforts to improve herself by study outside of school.

"Personality is probably the most difficult quality to rate, but there are details of personality to which the city is certainly entitled to demand the attention of its teachers. One of these is neatness and fitness of dress. I have recently added to my collection of school curiosities the report upon a teacher who uses the class-room as a place in which to wear out the society dresses which she has shone in earlier in the season. The effect of these gowns she heightens by lavish displays of jewelry. Her girls, from poor homes, soon bloom out in extravagantly vulgar finery, with accompaniments of imitation jewels. None of us realize how much example and suggestion guides those placed in our charge. So far as I have been able to judge from the reports made to me the teachers of our school system are singularly appropriate in this regard. Where fault has been found it is in greatest proportion regarding the careless dress of men.

"The voice is certainly a personal feature that should be regarded in rating a teacher. We should not require children to listen five hours a day to a harsh, strident, disagreeable voice. It is every teacher's duty to cultivate a pleasing tone and a clear enunciation.

"Sympathy for children should be considered. When this is present gentleness is there also. When there is a feeling of hostility, a strife between the pupils and the class, rest assured that teacher is defective in personality. It is a matter of imagination. If the teacher will form the habit of imagining herself in the child's place she will come to see how much easier and pleasanter school work will be.

"Decision of character is an element of personality to be observed. We want teachers who will not announce a decision until well considered, but who will carry it out when made. Untruthfulness and injustice in teachers are unpardonable sins.

"In rating control of class the only kind of control to be marked meritorious is that obtained through interest in the work. Promise of reward is bad, fear and repression are worse. These means should be marked C or D. One phenomenon, where it is a class habit not seen or not cured by the teacher, should always be taken as evidence of unfit control, that is the repeated presentation of dishonest work by the pupils.

"Your general estimate of the teacher's ability need not be an average of your detailed marks. Bear in mind that the object of these ratings is not to fill columns with marks, but to do something to raise the teaching force of the city to a higher plane than it yet occupies."

Note.—For outline of this address, see *Methods in Education*, page 52.

Examinations as Tests of Fitness

372. **Examinations for admission.**—Many cities conduct examinations for licenses to teach, no matter what credentials the applicant may hold. The New York City examinations have been subjected to severe criticism at home and abroad. Teachers in the system have not spared their censure of superiors, nor have the hundreds of unsuccessful applicants spoken softly of the various requirements. But in this, as in all other phases of school organization, students should view the topic broadly and then fit themselves to meet the requirements which cannot be overthrown by debate. The affirmative of this discussion is presented by two members of the Board of Examiners

373. **By City Superintendent Maxwell.**

"Examinations, however, may be so conducted as to determine fitness very closely, certainly to exclude the grossly unfit. There must be both a written and oral examination, for a well-ordered written examination is an almost infallible test whether the examinee has the ability to marshal his resources at a sudden call, whether he can think clearly and coherently, whether he has an adequate mastery of written discourse, and whether he has the executive ability to adjust the task to the allotted time with due sense of proportion. All of these powers are powers which the skilful teacher ought to possess, and which may be fairly tested by a written examination.

374. "The written examination, to serve its purpose must, of course, be a test of whether or not the applicant has the knowledge, the power of thought and the facility of expression that a teacher ought to have. An examination that would test mere book knowledge or memory would be practically useless for the purpose in view.

375. "There are certain things that a written examination cannot determine. It is not a certain test of moral character, or of personal charm, cleanliness, address, or even of teaching power. It does not reveal bodily deformity, sickness, faulty enunciation or foreign accent. It is even within the limits of possibility that a man may write well who talks very badly, and hence is unfit for teaching work. To determine these matters other methods of examination must be resorted to. The other methods which we use in New York include:

376. "First, An oral examination given only to those whose marks in the written examination indicate that they are worthy of further consideration.

377. "Second, By the term 'oral examination' we mean not merely the presentation and answering of oral questions, but also an exhaustive investigation of the past history and present qualifications of the applicant, both personally and professionally. The ratio of the maximum record mark to the minimum oral mark varies according to the license sought. Some licenses require little or no

teaching for eligibility, as, for instance, the initial license. Other licenses require large teaching experience, and this experience must necessarily be made a matter of investigation.

378. "Written statements regarding teachers must be received and rated with the utmost care. They must be rated for what they do not say, no less for what they say. For instance, a principal of a normal school reports a pupil as 'good' in scholarship, as 'high' in pedagogical work, as 'good' in private teaching. At the close of her first year of work in New York the principal of the school to which she had been assigned reported that her imperfect knowledge and very deficient enunciation of the English language render her incompetent to control or interest any class in this department.

379. "This is only one sample out of hundreds which I might adduce to show that school authorities often use unnessarily roseate language in writing testimonials. Episodes of this kind have led the Board of Examiners to lay great stress upon what they term the 'oral examination.' They now lay such stress upon the mark on record, personality and ability to speak the English language that a bad mark in any one of these particulars nullifies the whole examination

380. "Turning from processes to results, I am happy to be able to report that recent investigations have shown:

381. "First, that those persons who have received the highest standings at our examination have, upon the whole, done better than those who

receive the lowest standings that were considered possible.

382. "Second, nine-tenths of those whom it has been necessary to dismiss at or before the close of the probationary term are to be found in the class of persons who received comparatively low standings at the examination.

383. "Third, the examinations have been the means of bringing to the New York schools many teachers of high character and ability from other places, whose services it would not have been possible to obtain in any other way. When it is known that the teachers in a city school system are appointed as the result of the competitive examination, honestly and skilfully conducted, the best teachers from all over the country will flock to that city."

384.   By Dr. Hervey, of Board of Examiners.

"The first advantage of the present system is fairness. In the written examination the personal identity of the applicant is not revealed to the examiner. All persons examined receive the same questions, are given the same time, and are judged with impartiality and leisure. The personal equation, both of the examiner and of the examined, is absolutely eliminated. The whole inquiry centers upon certain definite matters of knowledge and power—and those of great importance—considered apart from all other matters. It is evident that the written examination suffers decided limitations from this very fact, and yet in its limitations there undoubtedly lies a certain advantage.

385. "The second advantage is that of record. The examination paper written by the applicant's own hand is an original document. Its testimony, so far as it goes, is unimpeachable. Moreover, it may serve as a definite basis of appeal and reconsideration.

386. "With all its limitations a written examination is certainly a valid test of something. It shows at least whether the examinee has done what he was set to do; it shows probably whether he can do what he was set to do; it shows pretty accurately whether he has the power to adjust the task to the time with due sense of proportion; and whether he can marshal his resources and set forth what he knows in due order and form.

387. "That type of written examination will best serve as a test of professional fitness which most nearly approximates in its character the nature of the work to be done by the person passing the test. The written examination for a teacher's license must, as far as possible, be a test of whether or not the applicant has the knowledge, the judgment, and the power of thought and of expression that a teacher should have.

388. "The main use made of the written examination is to determine who shall not be permitted to proceed further in the examination It serves as a uniform and absolutely fair, level and practicable, though rough means of sifting the better from the worse.

389. "The written examination should always be, and in the practice of the Board of Examiners

always is, supplemented by an oral examination
which usually comes after the written marks are
known. It has been suggested that the oral examination should be given before the written. To this
plan the objections are: (1) The time of the board
would be wasted on absolutely undeserving candidates. (2) The oral examination is by its very nature a less conclusive and convincing test.

390. "The oral mark is the result of an exhaustive investigation of the past history and present
qualifications of the applicant, both personally and
professionally. In the case of certain licenses half
of the credits in the total oral mark are assigned to
the items of 'studies' and 'record and teaching
power,' predominance being naturally given to the
item of 'record and teaching power.' A person who
falls below the passing mark in record is counted
as having failed in the examination, however high
may have been his marks in the written examination and in the other items of the oral examination.

391. "The rest of the oral mark is made up of
the answers to questions in the oral examination
proper and the judgment of the examiners as to the
personality of the applicant. In the examination
for a certain license the ratio of personality to questions is as two to three, 30 out of 100 credits being
assigned to answers of oral questions.

392. "The reason for this is obvious. The conditions of a necessarily brief oral test preclude an
exhaustive investigation, and the preceding written
examination usually renders such investigation unnecessary. It sometimes happens that a person of

flawless record, who has passed a high written examination, and who has given satisfactory answers to oral questions, is weighed and found wanting on the sole ground of personality The forming of a judgment as to personality is an affair of the utmost delicacy and discrimination. In some cases it is easy enough to tell at sight, or otherwise, whether one applicant is or is not a clean gentleman; whether another is a gentlewoman or an ungentlewoman In other cases it is not so easy.

393. "The complaints from those who are kept out on personal grounds are as nothing compared with the righteous and justifiable indignation of principals and fellow teachers who are obliged to work with such objectionable persons as have, I grieve to say, been allowed, in comparatively small numbers, to slip into the system The answer of the Board of Examiners to such complains is that during the school year 1903-4 out of 231 applicants for License No 1 coming from a single institution all but 35, or nearly six-sevenths of the whole, were rejected, although only half of those applying failed in the written examination. In partly computing what's done it may be a comfort to remember what's resisted.

394. "It should be remembered also that the pressure for teachers is so great that the duty of the Board of Examiners becomes sometimes not to select those who are fit, or to reject all those who seem unfit, but to supply teachers for the schools.

395. "The maximum personality mark varies according to the license, from 15 to 20 per cent. of the

total. But of more importance than the per cent. accorded to it is the fact that this mark, too, as well as record and teaching power, possesses the veto power."

396. **Summary of tests of character and fitness of applicants.**—Here is an official summary of the tests used by the Board of Examiners in determining the character and the general fitness of applicants for the several licenses to teach in New York City   These tests are, of course, aside from the written examination.

1   Moral character, as indicated in the record of the applicant as a student or teacher or in other occupation, or as a participant in an examination.

2.   Physical fitness for the position sought; reference being had here to all questions of physical fitness other than those covered in the physician's report as to "sound health"

3.   Technical skill in special subjects, as music, drawing, etc.

4   Satisfactory quality and use of voice, and satisfactory command and reasonably correct use of language, whether in writing or in speech.

5.   Personal bearing, cleanliness, appearance, manners.

6.   Self-command and power to win and hold the respect of teachers, school authorities, and the community

7.   Capacity for school discipline, power to maintain order and to secure the willing obedience and the friendship of pupils.

8.   Teaching ability, as indicated by skill and

efficiency in explanation, in questioning, in use of blackboard and of objective illustration, in arousing the interest in the use of appreciation, etc.

9. Business or executive ability—power to comprehend and carry out and to accomplish prescribed work, school management, as relating to adjustment of desks, lighting, heating, ventilation, cleanliness, and attractiveness of school-room, handling of supplies, etc.

10. Capacity for supervision, for organization and administration of a school, and the instructing, assisting, and inspiring of teachers

The means employed in the inquiry as to the several points enumerated are written and oral examinations, class-room tests or observations, inspection of official records and of reports from persons named as references, or from other persons having information; interviews or hearings of applicants or others; correspondence

Conduct of the Recitation

397. **Purpose of the recitation.**—Hinsdale said that teaching is "bringing knowledge into due relation with the mind." That is one general purpose of the recitation; and, in a large sense, it is the purpose of the recitation to furnish all the opportunities that educate Specifically, the recitation period is a time for ascertaining what the pupils have acquired under assigned lessons, what difficulties have been encountered, and what the teacher must do to help pupils acquire effectual habits of study. It is

a time for the meeting of the minds,—the achievement most desirable in teaching. Compare section 75; consult index in this book and in McEvoy's *Answers in School Management*.

398. **Methods of the recitation.**—This topic suggests inductive-deductive method, topical method, heuristic questioning, empirical to rational, and many other familiar terms in examination questions and pedagogical discussions. For consideration in the science of education, let the student hold to the interdependence of personality of teacher, subject-matter, and methods of teaching. The three form a unity in efficient teaching but each may be considered alone in educational classification. Use chapter VII, pages 76 to 98, in *Methods in Education* for adequate description of the respective methods in elementary work, and then apply chosen kinds in higher instruction. The desirability of any method may be measured by the initiative aroused and the reactions produced in the pupils.

399. **Concert recitation.**—Most of the teaching must necessarily be directed to the class as a whole, since our systems of grading aim to associate pupils who are approximately uniform in ability and capacity. This statement applies to all acts of instruction, whether called presentation, drill or review. But this does not mean, however, that concert recitation is approved for regular use. The whole class should be ready to answer when one is asked to recite; otherwise, the minds are not united in the act of learning. Concert recitation is good

for arousing class animation occasionally, for united thought in rapid reviews, and for developing school spirit in quotations, memory selections and songs; but as a daily recitation plan, it is censured in section 371.

400. **Group teaching.**—This device in class management is a valuable concession to pupils, since the welfare of pupils is put above the claims of rigid grading. It indicates respect for individuality by trying to adapt the whole scheme of education to each pupil's capacity. It is commendable, furthermore, because it can be put into use in any grade or subject throughout the whole course of education.

Group teaching is not new although many of its adaptations may be It means, of course, dividing the class into groups, according to ability, so that three groups, for example, shall be working on three respective kinds of assignment at the same time during one period. The teacher may be giving oral instruction to one group, while the other two are engaged in written exercises.

Eight arguments in favor of group teaching are given on pages 60 and 61 of *Methods in Education.* Supplement that reasoning by arranging a series of lessons for group work in some subject in secondary education

401. **Individual teaching.**—No matter what devices or methods or novelties may be advocated, the process of true teaching remains a personal relation between the teacher and individual pupils. The most successful class or group teaching is that in ·which the individuals in the class or group are able

to put their minds into sympathetic communication with the teacher's mind, or vice versa. When the successful pupils have passed along with the satisfaction of a good degree of mastery, slow or defective pupils remain for individual teaching to give them the right of promotion When any pupil fails to understand the instruction, when disorder interferes with the smooth course of teaching, when illness or other valid excuse causes absence, then there must be a personal meeting of the minds of teacher and pupil to restore conditions to a normal standard of efficiency So under all circumstances it is safe to argue that individual teaching is the largest factor in the school education

Grading and Promotion

402. **A general problem.**—The transition from grammar schools to high schools has been attended by many serious difficulties. Teachers in high schools have gone so far as to make a sweeping condemnation of methods and results in the elementary schools. Pupils entering high schools are said to be deficient in matter, power of oral and written expression, habits of study, capacity for adaptation, and desire for knowledge Is this criticism valid, or is there a distinctively different attitude in high school teaching? There is failure in adjustment somewhere in the course, since hundreds of boys and girls fail to complete two years of study after graduation from the grammar school. Is promotion forced? Are courses of study flexible enough?

Is personality of teacher or pupil sacrificed to external form? Does real education reach the individual? Let us have your answer

403. **Pueblo plan.**—While group teaching is an approach to individual instruction, we find a still more definite attempt in this line in the plan adopted in Pueblo, Colorado, and known as the Pueblo Plan This plan is only the other extreme in the hope of avoiding the defects of classification and gradation. *The Educational Review*, February, 1894, has this paragraph about the Pueblo Plan:

"The fundamental characteristic of the plan on which the schools are organized is its conservation of the individual. The pupil is placed purely with reference to where he can get the most good for himself; he works as an individual, progresses as an individual, is promoted as an individual, and is graduated as an individual The ordinary nomenclature of schools is continued for convenience; but the school system is one of flexibility, permitting pupils to pass from working-section to working-section as may be expedient. The perplexities relative to class intervals have disappeared, because there is no mechanical classification. In appellation the term junior or senior may be used, but such term does not locate the individual any more than the name of a division of a railroad locates the exact position of a particular train. For working purposes the pupils are grouped in working sections; but the members of a working-section are not necessarily doing the same work, or rather they are not doing the same work simultaneously. In brief, the school is both graded and ungraded,—graded in so far as applies to its plan of work, but ungraded in its accommodations of the individual."

Comment on this plan in contrast to the fixed plan. Apply to high school work

404. Batavia plan.—See page 62 in *Methods in Education* for a terse description.

The summary of an address delivered by Superintendent Kennedy before the department of Educational Science of Cornell University on June 16, 1904, puts in concise form twelve propositions that are worthy of serious study. Take 9 and 10, for instance, and test the foregoing sections in this chapter.

1. "Schools become clogged, (*a*) by slow minds, (*b*) by irregular attendance, (*c*) by discouraged minds.

2. "The attempt to force forward an obstructed school is detrimental to all concerned. (*a*) It overstrains the teacher. (*b*) It depresses the teaching. (*c*) It destroys the condition of repose and equipoise essential to good teaching (*d*) It is wasteful of time, destructive of interest, and promotive of discouragement. (*e*) It tends to wholesale failure, indicated by the great multitude who drop out, and by the indifferent scholarship of the few who persevere to the end.

3 "Statistics show that in elementary and in secondary schools, and throughout the first stages of higher education, the falling out is the rule and that a low grade of work and scholarship is the

rule with those who remain. Hence failure is the rule, and high success the minute exception

4. "The clogging of schools may be practically, if not entirely, relieved, by devoting half the teaching force to individual instruction. (*a*) By directing attention definitely to the point where the pinch or clog occurs. (*b*) By operating upon the difficulty according to its exact nature and without resort to any kind of force.

5. "Individual attention involves no strain on the teacher and no violence to the pupil, hence it tends to that condition of repose and equipoise essential to good teaching and to successful study

6. "Individual teaching tends to check all lagging and flagging, whether resulting from discouragement or lack of interest, and to promote a general forward movement in the student ranks. (*a*) It sustains the interest of the brighter pupils by permitting them to move on, and by doing away with the irksome deadlocks, repetitions and tragic struggles of the recitation   (*b*) It brings forward the slower pupils by recognizing their real trouble, by saving them from public exposure and persecution, by gently leading them back from chaos to where the ground is solid under their feet. by giving them direction, and by awakening within them confidence in their own powers.

7. "Individual instruction is quite as potent and essential in the moral as in the intellectual training of youth. (*a*) The will to do what is right and wholesome is an expression of moral health. (*b*) Failure tends to unsettle character and to per-

vert the will. Under failure there is a giving way of either physical or moral health, sometimes of both.

8. "Individual instruction is a definitely restricted agency in the education of youth. (*a*) Its function is strictly remedial; it addresses itself solely to disturbed conditions (*b*) Its end is attained in the restoration of desirable conditions (*c*) It brings about its own elimination and gives way when the conditions for exclusive class instruction are ideal.

9. "Class instruction is the normal and permanent form of the best education of youth. It supplies (*a*) the spur of emulation, (*b*) the stimulus of numbers, (*c*) the attrition of mind upon mind, (*d*) the sidelights from many minds, (*e*) a greater breadth of teaching than can be given to an individual, and (*f*) an experience in thinking and doing in the presence of a public

10 "Only through the restorative effects of individual instruction can a school reach anything like ideal conditions for class work, and only through the constant operation of individual instruction can those conditions be maintained. Therefore, individual instruction is a constantly necessary phase of school activity, the constant and necessary supplement and corrective of class teaching.

11. "Individual instruction involves no increase of labor or expense in the education of youth, but rather the reduction of both

12. "Finally, statistics show that schools pro-

vided with systematic individual instruction carry
their pupils to higher stages of advancement and
give them sounder scholarship than do schools
which lack this agency. In other words, these statistics emphasize the fact that the business of education is to educate, and not to evade its responsibilities by seeking lines of least resistance."

405. **High school aided by Batavia plan.**—We
quote from Superintendent Kennedy's report to
Batavia Board of Education.

"We continue to have a very large increase in
our High School and upper grades, and in the educational results reached. This increase is out of
all proportion to the natural growth of the town
and of the primary grades. This expansion at the
top has been going on steadily for the past four
years, or since we incorporated individual instruction into our scheme of education I think that
this increase at the top indicates a restoration of
conditions that were disturbed by pure class-teach-
ing. It represents an element saved from failure.
The attendance in our High School will soon be
doubled as a result of this saving, whereas the increase in our first primary grade will not reach 20
per cent. These facts are convincing us that the
dropping out of children and young people is not
due entirely, nor even mainly, to necessity. It is
due mainly to the discouragement, failure and
physical breakdown promoted by educating *en
masse*. We are convinced that by a due amount of
individual instruction, combined with a proper
amount of class work, we are taking away all the

strain and health-destroying worry that have been but too common in our graded-school system. And we are convinced that we are building up health, confidence, efficiency and ambition."

406. **School evils banished.**—The point of interest in the Batavia plan is the transfer of opportunity to the pupil. The teachers direct the activity, and soon the pupil's consciousness of progress turns self-activity toward self-realization. That is real teaching, directive effort is centered upon the pupil, not upon external organization. Other cities tried the Batavia plan, but some experimenters were dissatisfied. Among the satisfactory reports is one from Superintendent Holmes, of Westerley, Rhode Island. He finds, among other things, that nagging and scolding disappear and teachers and pupils become cheerful and happy; there is such cheerful obedience to lawful authority that stern methods of discipline become unnecessary; there is no detention after school for discipline; all work is done in the school-room; when school is out the children are free, pupils are all promoted; the attendance in upper grammar grades and high schools is nearly as good as in the primary grades, the high-school population increasing to a remarkable degree, the dull and backward pupil is shown to possess superior mental powers; the laggard is made a leader; and stumbling blocks are converted into stepping stones.

407. **Home lesson.**—For arguments for and against, see *Methods in Education*, page 64.

Corporal Punishment

408. **Viewpoint.**—The tendency throughout the civilized world is toward the prohibition of corporal punishment. The abuse of the privilege is one reason for prohibitory laws, but a far better reason is a growing belief that the use of corporal punishment makes *fear* the source of order, whereas *interest* should lead through the self-activity of the child to a habit of permanent self-control. This theoretical perfection of character harmonizes with the theory of moral training in New York City The positive effort substitutes desirable habits for undesirable tendencies, and thus the negative is not made unduly emphatic. To enforce this viewpoint, study pages 65 to 76 in *Methods in Education.*

409. **Suggestion.**—Make an outline that you would be willing to follow in discussing punishment. See any good text on school management, McEvoy's *Answers in School Management,* or chapter XXIV in Dexter and Garlick's *Psychology.*

410. **An old view.**—Discuss the following quotation. "Punishment must naturally follow the offense and be proportioned to it "

The old view of this doctrine permitted the teacher to get even with the pupil for every breach of discipline Retribution had a prominent place in punishment. External means were applied to the external side of the offense, although such punishment in many cases tended to aggravate it If a boy played truant for a day it was considered proper to force him to stay after school long enough

to make up for the number of hours he had missed
on account of his truancy. If a girl annoyed her
teacher by whispering, that girl had to endure an
equivalent amount of annoyance in some other
form from the teacher. In both these cases the
punishment failed to reach the source of the offense, namely, the *will* of the pupil. If the school
is a spiritual unity, forming a part of organized
society, it should look to the spiritual cause of the
offense and apply a spiritual remedy. This idea is
made prominent in *School Management*, by Tompkins. Quotation follows

"An offense, then, is the action of the will, on
the part of either pupil or teacher, which negatives
the will creating and sustaining the school,—the
will as embodied in, and interpreted by, the teacher
and school officers. It is the individual's purpose
set counter to the whole This makes the application of the law clear. If correction, or punishment,
naturally follows the offense, it is by an action of
the will in the offender; and if it be proportioned
to the offense, it must completely reverse the wrong
action of the will The pupil who breaks the spiritual unity of the school by choosing against it, must
reverse that choice before he has cancelled his offense. This makes his punishment naturally follow
the offense, and proportions it to the offense; for
he simply undoes his wrong act, and thereby restores himself to the institution. The pupil alone
has the power to sever his connection with the
school; and he alone has the power to reinstate
himself when once out. No mechanical process

can restore the pupil whose mind is at variance with the institution; he must reinstate himself by changing his spiritual attitude

"Thus briefly we have suggested how to restore the unity when broken: The pupil who breaks the unity must, by his own act of mind, restore it. And the law of punishment at the outset means just this: the deed being in the will, the punishment must be there too, and when the will has cancelled its own deed, the punishment is exactly proportioned to the offense. Anything beyond this is gratuitous on the part of the teacher, and an aggression on the rights of the pupil. The idea of retribution is thus excluded."

Self-Government

411. Student self-government.—Think of the features and the limitations Such plans are in operation in both elementary and high schools in this city. See chapter VII, Dutton's *School Management*

412. School cities.—A new development of the public school system is being tested in New York, Philadelphia and some New England cities. It is the establishment of "School Cities," with the basic principle of self-government, on the line of the government of the United States

The first "City School" was established in the Norfolk Street School, New York, in 1897, by Wilson L. Gill, as an experiment. In 1898 the Philadelphia school board introduced the system as an experiment, and now has thirty-three "school cities" in as many different schools

The U. S. Government was so impressed by the idea that in 1900 Mr. Gill was sent to Cuba to introduce the school city into the schools of the new republic during the American occupancy, and the following two years he organized 800 "school cities" in the island

A National School City League was organized a few weeks ago in Washington, which aims to gather in all the scattered elements interested and to push the organization of school cities vigorously. Mr. Gill has been retained as national organizer and lecturer, and various organizations have been asked to lend their influence to the movement.

The interest aroused may be judged by the response of the Massachusetts Federation of Women's Clubs. This body recently appointed a committee to push the movement until a school city shall be organized in every city of Massachusetts.

Mr. Gill points out the object of the "school city" in this manner:

"There are sometimes boards, sometimes not. In all details of government the school city tries to follow the government of the larger city in which it is located," he said.

"The school city is not a mimic government, but a miniature government Did you ever stop to think that while the American child is destined to take his place in a democratic government he is brought up under an autocracy? He has autocratic government at home, he has autocratic government at school. The rule of his parents may be too indulgent or too severe, but in either case it is government imposed upon him from without.

"He goes to school and finds another autocratic force ready to impose government upon him. If it were not for the rough and tumble democracy which the children get among themselves they would all grow up little serfs. As it is, the preeminent lesson taught them by every form of government with which they come in contact, from parent to policeman, is respect for authority.

"Now, respect for authority is right and necessary in its place, but it is not the American ideal. It is an Oriental ideal The American ideal is self-government, a finding out of the right thing to do and then doing it of your own accord because it is best for all concerned

"These are the ideals of democracy, unattained though they may be And it is wonderful to see how well and easily the children carry them out in the school city, and what a difference self-government makes in their attitude toward rules.

"They readily make laws concerning punctuality, for instance. They are perfectly capable of seeing that the class work will be broken up if members are to come in whenever they please. They will hold court and pass on cases of tardiness, elucidating the cause and deciding on penalties with the utmost gravity and fairness.

"In the Daniel L. Keyser School of Philadelphia, the first arrests were made for profanity in the school yard. This was a surprise to the teachers, for they did not know such offenses were being committed The judge in each case sentenced the offender not to speak to any person at recess time for a stated period, and every pupil in school seemed actively interested in seeing that the order of the court was carried out Such sending to coventry would probably never have occurred to a teacher, and had a teacher imposed such a sentence it is probable that the pupils would have taken no trouble to execute it

"One arrest was for trying to pick a fight because of an unintentional provocation. The sentence was to copy neatly and carefully twenty times the first law of the school city code, which was:

"Do unto others as you wish them to do to you. This is the natural law, without which no popular government can succeed, and it is the general law of this School City, to which all other laws and regulations must conform

"The ambition to hold an office to which they have been elected by their fellow citizens is a most potent influence in the school city, and the influence of an office in transforming the conduct and even the appearance of some pupils has been very marked.

"Any other art, trade, occupation or profession whatever, we spend time and effort to teach our children if we expect them to know it But the art of living in a democratic community, the art of self-government, we give them not a hint of.

"We let them come up under totally autocratic government, we give them not a glimpse into the practical workings of popular government, and when they are of voting age they are ripe for gang rule and blind partisanship."

The new national School City League has William L. Gill, Franklin Institute, Philadelphia, as its president; Ralph Albertson, Jamaica Plain, Boston, secretary; and George H Shibley, Bliss Building, Washington, treasurer.—*Maryland Educational Journal*, October 15, 1905

413. References.

ARNOLD   *School and Class Management.*

BAGLEY.   *School Room Management.*

DUTTON.   *School Management.*

LANDON.   *School Management.*

McEVOY   *Answers in School Management.*

PERRY   *The Management of a City School.*

WHITE   *School Management*

CHAPTER XIII

APPROVED SET OF ANSWERS

This set of High School questions is answered by a person in authority. While no two candidates would answer exactly alike, this paper furnishes a model which is approved by the Board of Examiners. This was an examination in the Science of Education applied to English as a specialty. Time, three hours.

413. *State three tests (aside from reviews or examinations) which may enable a teacher to estimate a pupil's understanding of the class work   Illustrate these three tests.*

In English teaching an estimate may be made of a pupil's understanding of class work by the following three tests: Interest, the Recitation, and Growth of power

1   **Interest.**—Interest grows out of apperception.   If the pupil is deeply interested in class work we have evidence that he understands it, since it is impossible to be interested long in what we do not comprehend.   Interest has been employed as a test of successful teaching for many years in the evening schools of New York City.   It has been the custom to discharge teachers if their attendance fell below a certain figure   As Evening

School attendance is entirely voluntary, the power to hold a class together for a season of six months is almost entirely a question of interesting the pupils by successful teaching.

2. **The Recitation.**—The recitation is primarily a teaching instrument but it is also incidentally a test. Unskillful teachers usually reverse these two offices, using the recitation primarily as a test and only incidentally to teach. The good teacher needs hardly any other test than the recitation to measure the fidelity and success of his pupils. If they are interested, they will reveal their interest in the attention they give to the recitation and the pleasure they derive from it. The answers they give to questions; the remarks they contribute in discussions; the questions they ask; the fidelity with which they prepare their written exercises, perform experiments and record observations, are all data whereby the progress of children may be accurately gauged.

3. **Growth of Power.**—The third test of the pupil's success is his growth in power. The teacher who tests all children by a uniform dead-level of results achieved is liable to do injustice to pupils, while he misinforms himself. For instance: The writer recently heard a fourth-year class read in a third reader. Most of the pupils read very fluently, and seemed to understand perfectly what they read. Finally one little boy got up who read haltingly and enunciated very indistinctly and inaccurately. On inquiry it transpired that this child had come from Italy only eleven months before. Judged by

the absolute standard of success he had failed in his reading utterly; but judged by his growth in power he made a brilliant recitation

Teachers often take credit to themselves for the success of very bright pupils, when, as a matter of fact, they deserve no thanks at all Unless every pupil shows progress the teacher has not been entirely successful. A pupil is doing good work only if he can show progress daily, weekly, monthly, all along the line of his educational endeavor

414. *What is the imagination? State with reasons your views as to the importance of cultivation of the imagination as a part of education. How may the imagination be developed through the study of your specialty? Illustrate*

Imagination.—Imagination is the power of forming mental images by uniting different parts or qualities of objects given by perception. It also has the power of creating ideals of objects different from anything we have perceived An image is a revived percept of any kind An idea is any product of the representative power, whether percept or concept. (Sully).

Imagination involves reproduction and production. It revives our past experience and works it up into new products. In producing the new it has the power to change the form of the material and its relations to time and place and circumstances There are several kinds of imagination. Phantasy is a play of ideas uncontrolled by the laws of thought or of probability. All dreams come under this head; so also do caricatures and grotesque ideas such as we find in Baron Munchausen, Alice in Wonderland, and certain stories of Kipling Fancy is a little higher than phantasy, and involves more regulation of the process by the power of will Longfellow's comparison of the moon to a paper kite is a fancy. Young children and young poets incline to the fanciful.

Creative Imagination.—Creative imagination is the voluntary process of combining images into new forms Its products are ideals Idealization is the process of fixing the attention upon the most satisfying example of the actual, and withdrawing the attention from its defects, until it stands before the mind as an ideal example In this way the imagination idealizes the forms of space to create geometry In art the Greek masterpieces are ideals, in religion Christ is an ideal of moral perfection.

The principal duty of the teacher in regard to the imagination of children is to guide the fancy and gradually to transform it into creative imagination. This is done by supplying suitable exercises and materials for creative work.

The importance of imagination in the life of a child may be readily appreciated when we reflect that play is nearly the whole of his spontaneous activity. A child's mental life is thus as rich as the adult's. What he lacks of experience as an organ of apperception, fancy supplies. He sees in his rude toys a thousand attributes and actions with which his imagination endows them.

The higher forms of imagination are modes of

apperception. All literature is the product of imagination. The difference between good prose which is not literature and prose which is literature, is the element contributed by the imagination. One may readily see this difference by comparing a passage from Sewell or Ruskin with a paragraph from an ordinary scientific work.

Such being the character of literature, it is one of the very best subjects for cultivating the imagination of children. This cultivation may be brought about by the critical and appreciative study of masterpieces and by imitations and original compositions of a similar character. Especially important is the use of the imagination in the ethical life of the child. Sympathy and other altruistic sentiments depend largely upon the power of imagination. Imagination gives value and dignity to human existence. Without it life is poor and barren and sordid; with it we are able to find "tongues in trees, books in the running brooks, sermons in stones, and good in everything."

415. (a) *State in the order of importance what you regard as the three main objects or ends to be kept in view by the high school teacher Give reasons for your arrangement* (b) *State how the teaching of your subject may be used toward these ends*

(a) The objects of secondary education may be variously conceived and expressed Perhaps as good a summary as any of these ends is the following: Interest, Culture, Freedom

Interest.—In offering interest as a school end, we are following the Herbartians, who would say that the object of all teaching is to give the pupil an appetite for knowledge. If we do not succeed in creating such a desire for further light we have no guarantee that the pupil will continue his education after school days are over.

Culture.—The secondary school dates from the Renaissance It has always stood for culture and discipline. There is a strong effort to make it a utility school on the part of many teachers and laymen, who insist that education must be "practical." The two-year commercial course in the High school is a result of this movement. But the friends of true education have stood firm thus far and the High school as a typical institution has a stiff course of purely culture studies. The teacher is to set up this aim as one of the goals of his instruction. Facts, formal studies, recitations, all school exercises, yield their true value only if they give the pupil culture. By culture is meant training, development, refinement of mind, morals and taste.

Freedom.—The third object of secondary teaching is freedom—intellectual and moral independence. Hence the aim of the teacher must be to emancipate the pupil from the necessity of supervision. This is accomplished by compelling him to perform for himself set tasks, by training in observation and the exact methods of science, and by independent book study. Moral freedom is attained by self-control. The discipline therefore must assume that the pupil is a rational being who is able and willing to do right. So far as possible he is to be left to his honor and sense of what is right Repressive measures must be eliminated and constant appeal to the better instincts and growing promptings of conscience substituted

The moral freedom is the supreme aim; it is therefore placed last "The term virtue expresses the whole purpose of education." These are the opening words of Herbart's famous "Outlines of Educational Doctrine." Culture ranks next in importance. For this reason it is placed second. He who has culture is first a man, with cultivated mind, able to use his powers for the benefit of mankind in whatever direction he chooses to apply himself.

(b) It is not difficult to surmise how literature may be used to secure the ends thus set forth. Interest is secured by giving the pupil literary works adapted to this capacity, of such transcendent merit that he will want to read more of the same sort. The methods of study is to be heuristic. The pupil must study and appreciate the actual books, rather than learn things about books Thus will he get the culture which is the second aim of study. There is no other subject so well adapted as literature to train children in ethical purpose. The contents of all literary works is ethical Hence the study of such works is training in ethical insight, and all such training leads to that moral freedom which is the supreme end of education.

416. *Answer* (a) *or* (b). (a) *What are the most noteworthy features of the views on education of the following writers Milton, Ruskin, Spencer?* (b) *What three writers do you regard as the most notable innovators in the history of education since 1600? What in*

substance did each contribute to the development of modern education?

(*b*) The three most notable innovators in education since 1600 were, doubtless, Rousseau (1712-1778), Pestalozzi (1746-1827), and Froebel (1783-1852). It is not contended that they necessarily invented or discovered the greatest number of new devices or principles of education; but judged by the influence which they exerted upon the progress of modern education, they tower above all other figures in the history of the period.

1. **Rousseau.**—Rousseau represented a movement called Romanticism, of which his theories of education were but an incident. A large group of philosophers and another of literary artists formed a part of this phase of human progress. One of its cardinal principles was the enthusiasm for nature and for naturalism in art and life, as opposed to the artificialities in vogue when the movement originated. Rousseau's political theories were even more important than his educational doctrine, for to these is commonly attributed the French Revolution and the modern passion for political freedom. As a man Rousseau was thoroughly detestable. He was a shameless rake, a man with no consistent principle of rectitude or honor, an erratic genius. But he was a genius and hence, partly because the times were ripe for a man of his type, his influence upon education has been prodigious.

Rousseau knew little or nothing of the art of schoolmastering The Emilie is simply an application of Rousseau's principles of society and life to education. The scheme outlined is thoroughly impracticable, often ridiculous, sometimes immoral, and would produce instead of civilized beings, a generation of monstrosities. But in spite of these defects, the author has hit, as if by instinct, upon many of the profoundest educational truths, and has expressed and illustrated them with a force and a charm which make his works immortal.

2. **Pestalozzi.**—Part of Rousseau's influence is due to the great men he stimulated to apply his principles in a rational way to elementary education.

It was Rousseau's *Contrat Social* which made Pestalozzi give up the theological career to which he had intended to devote himself. And thus Pestalozzi became the missionary of public elementary education. What Kant is to modern philosophy, Pestalozzi is to modern pedagogy Pestalozzi's work is the foundation of the modern public school; for prior to his day, in spite of Luther's great work and Francke's, and Rochow's, popular education, as we now understand it, did not exist. The history of the common school during the nineteenth century is largely the history of Pestalozzianism. The essence of this new doctrine is that the gospel of education has been preached to the poor, and that the schoolmaster is exhorted to discard his dead and abstract formulas, and bring the child in contact with realities It is, after all, merely the theory of Rousseau, but it is worked out in detail and propagated by a humane, God-fearing, fatherly missionary, whose enthusiasm enkindles a continent.

3. **Froebel.**—Froebel in his turn, was inspired by Pestalozzi, and the kindergarten, which stands to his credit, is a concrete form of Rousseau's doctrine of naturalism as embodied in the beginnings of education. Education by play, it will be seen, is but the recognition of the principle of naturalism; for play is the very life of the infant.

Froebel's greatness is growing. We are just beginning to realize the possibilities of the kindergarten. And the principles of the kindergarten are applicable to all elementary education, and have largely transformed the primary school

417. *In what ways and to what extent has the advance in natural science, physical or psychological, during the last half century influenced the teaching of your subject? Specify changes that have taken place during the period mentioned, in the method of teaching your subject*

The advance in psychology during the last half century has profoundly influenced the teaching of English, as it has that of all other subjects. The old psychology was introspective and considered the mental life entirely from the adult point of view. The thoughts and feelings and experiences of the psychologist were read into the minds of children, and as a consequence false methods of teaching were evolved. Since the publication of Fechner's epoch-making book on psycho-physics, psychological research has followed more and more closely the quantitative methods of physical science and has given us body of fact, and principles on the life and development of children by which educational theory and practice have been revolutionized.

Among the changes in English teaching which a better understanding of the child mind has brought about are the following·

1   It is demonstrated that the process of learning involves a passing from the whole to parts and from parts to the whole. The normal method is to begin with the whole. Expressed in other terms, learning consists of two complementary phases, analysis and synthesis. Analysis is always first, but the process is never complete without the synthetic half Applied to the teaching of reading, these principles make it plain that the alphabetic method is wrong, since it begins with the parts and by acts of synthesis proceeds to the whole, which is the word or sentence Hence we have had many new ways of teaching reading, nearly all of which begin with the word or sentence and proceed by analysis to the parts or letters. Methods of reading, whose advertised merit is that they are "synthetic," are therefore to be strongly suspected.

2   Another reform of great consequence has taken place during the past fifteen years in the teaching of reading The movement had its origin in the conviction on the part of President Eliot and others that reading was too formal; that reading is but a means and not an end, and that so soon as the mechanical elements are mastered it should be used as a vehicle to transmit the contents of literature to the child. This reform, which was greatly assisted by the discussions and reports of the *Committee of Ten* and the *Committee of Fifteen*, has revo-

lutionized the school readers and the courses of study throughout the length and breadth of the land. Courses of study in the elementary school now demand, in the upper grades, the critical and appreciative study of masterpieces of literature, and the school readers are no longer made up of "useful information" and twaddle on moral subjects invented by the compilers of readers But they contain, even in the lowest numbers, pieces that possess genuine literary merit So that instead of reading about "Jane's Doll" and "Jack's Top," the boys and girls of the second and third grades read the poems of Longfellow, Field and Cary.

In the secondary and collegiate courses similar changes have occurred Formerly, courses in literature consisted largely of the mastery of treatises about literature and its creators. Now they consist of the concrete, first-hand study of entire masterpieces representing authors or types of literary form

The changes may be summed up by saying that the courses in English have been infinitely enriched by placing the emphasis on the subject-matter of literature rather than on the mere form of mechanical aspect.

418. *Explain the following terms. Manual training, Correlation, Culture Epoch Theory, Humanism, The Formal Steps in Instruction.*

Manual Training.—Manual training as used in modern educational writings, means usually manumental training, or the training of the mind through muscular expression It is supposed that there is no mental activity without a corresponding brain action. Brain activity is localized. Certain areas of the cortex are devoted to special functions. Thus there is the motor area, whence are controlled all voluntary muscular movements, the intellectual area, and some known centers devoted to the various senses. It is contended that if a child has only intellectual exercises, and little or no work involving the larger muscles, only a portion of the brain is exercised Hence all forms of construction are looked upon as means of exercising the motor area of the brain. Exercise demands increased circulation, and this means increased nutrition. Hence work in iron, wood and clay, as well as sewing and cooking, are looked upon as the expression of thought in three dimensions. They are, therefore, manumental training

Correlation.—Correlation means many things To Harris it means the adaptation of the child to his environment. This is accomplished by revealing to him nature and human nature through five subjects, which are regarded as windows of the soul. These are mathematics, geography, grammar, literature, history. Usually, correlation means the studying of things that are closely related in such a way that they mutually help each other; as, for example, history and geography. Some writers, like Parker and the Herbartians, prefer concentration as the generic term to represent the notion of correlation. Parker and Herbart, however, have nothing in common except the name.

The Culture Epoch Theory.—The culture epoch

theory of the Herbartians and others assumes that there is such a thing as psychogenesis, that is, that the individual child repeats in his mental development the steps that have been taken by the development of man as a species Taking certain typical stages of development like Egypt, Greece, Rome, etc , this theory assumes that the culture material selected from these civilizations fit more or less accurately different stages in the development of children. The course of study is, therefore, selected in accordance with the principle of psychogenesis

Humanism.—Humanism is that theory of education which believes with Pope that "the proper study of mankind is man." Many things in this ·world are worth knowing, but the knowledge of most worth is knowledge of man and of his thoughts and creations. The theory claims that science has no ethical contents, that its facts are non-moral Ethical insight can only be cultivated by the study of literature and history, where the motives of human action are laid bare, and the evolution of institutional life is exhibited

The Formal Steps.—The formal steps are the parts which the Herbartians say are necessary to a complete recitation. These steps grow out of Herbart's admirable analysis of the process of apperception. Writers differ as to the number of necessary steps, but the numbers usually given range from three to five DeGarmo enumerates four stages, as follows: (1) Preparation; (2) Presentation; (3) Formulation, (4) Application.

CHAPTER XIV

QUESTIONS AND TYPICAL ANSWERS

419. Types of answers.—The questions in this chapter are from the examinations for license to teach in the high schools in New York City. The answers are such as would be accepted on examinations of this kind. Some answers are more comprehensive than the answers that could be written under a time limit of three hours, but our purpose is to give enough to satisfy students whose time for preparation is limited. The memorizing verbatim is not advised; study, reflection and practice in written expression are the steps for all who wish to be exponents of education as development

On Education

420. Meaning of education.—"To prepare us for complete living is the function which education has to discharge. * * * It behooves us to set before ourselves, and ever to keep clearly in view, complete living as the end to be achieved; so that in bringing up our children we may choose subjects and methods of instruction with deliberate reference to this end."—*Herbert Spencer.*

"Education has for its aim the development of the powers of man,"—*Standard Dictionary.*

194

Explain what is implied in these two views of education, contrast them, and indicate the effect of applying each.

ANSWER   Believing, as he did, that the education prevailing in his time was an aimless survival of traditionalism, Herbert Spencer undertook to set instruction on a firm foundation by answering the question, "What knowledge is of most worth?" and making that answer the basis of his system Now with him, the value of any knowledge depended on its relation to "complete living" in the widest sense. Accordingly he undertook to determine the relative value of different kinds of knowledge, by their bearing on the various activities of life. These activities he defined in the order of their importance, as activities relating to (1) direct self-preservation; (2) indirect self-preservation (i. e. earning a living); (3) the rearing and discipline of children; (4) social and political relations, and (5) the cultivation of the tastes and feelings Taking up each of the activities in turn, he attempted to prove that natural science is the best instrument for developing it.

Further, classifying knowledge as being of value (1) intrinsic, (2) quasi-intrinsic and (3) conventional, he contended that the facts and principles of natural science were of the greatest intrinsic value, while the worth of the subjects mainly taught was merely conventional; as for instance,

Latin verse-making, or the biographies of kings and queens.

Again, considering mental acquirement for its worth (1) as knowledge, and (2) as discipline, he argued that the knowledge which possessed the greatest intrinsic value, was also, by a wise economy of nature, the best instrument of mental discipline. For instance, he would say that the making of Latin verse, worthless by any standard of intrinsic value, could not be defended as mental discipline, when some other study, e. g., physics, of high intrinsic worth, possessed a greater disciplinary value, as dealing with facts systematically related and serving to develop the logical memory. In brief, Mr. Spencer's view was an apotheosis of natural science, as Butler called it.

The second definition is not opposed to Herbert Spencer's when understood in the highest sense, for, according to him, natural science, which prepares for complete living, is also the best agent for developing the powers of the mind. This second definition seems to emphasize the idea for studies for discipline apart from their value for practical living. Liberally interpreted, this latter definition may be understood to mean education as Butler defines it, "a gradual adjustment to the spiritual possessions of the race; the five inheritances of the child, scientific, literary, aesthetic, institutional and religious." The definition puts the studies which develop the emotions, imagination, and will, on a level with those which mainly cultivate the judgment. It is the ideal and cultural aspect of education in contrast with the practical and utilitarian view of Herbert Spencer

The field of education is broad enough for both these views   Each must be used to correct and interpret the other   The former must make a place for literature, music and art on the same level with anatomy and physics, else it would tend to reduce education to a sort of mechanico-mental engineering.   The latter, while exalting the spiritual and aesthetic aspects of education, must not lose sight of the fundamental activities of human life, without which there can be reared no superstructure of the highest culture.

421.   **Meaning of education.**

The proximate aim of education, I take it, is to make the child, within himself, strong and self-reliant; in his experience, sensible and thorough; in his work, cheerful and earnest; in his attitude towards others, sympathetic and helpful; in short, to lead him to individual, social and universal efficiency —*IV N Hailman*

(*a*) *Discuss this view of education in the light of your own study and experience, criticising it favorably and adversely, if you have adverse criticisms*

(*b*) *What is the meaning of social "efficiency"?*

(*c*) *Enumerate other desirable aims of education as given in definitions you have studied*

ANSWER.   The consciousness of self-development or self-realization has long been an aim of true education.   This consciousness does produce strength and self-reliance, because it is the result of victory over difficulties.

The view of education given in the above quotation might be criticised as failing to bring out the idea of race inheritance.

(a) Social efficiency means the development of that power or powers in the individual which will make him most useful in the group or class to which he belongs

(b) Horne speaks of the "superior adjustment of the individual to his environment" as the great aim of education

Butler brings out the need of giving to each individual his spiritual inheritance by which he means, the scientific, literary, institutional, religious and aesthetic possessions of the race.

Spencer makes "complete living" the aim. This he explains as follows. "Complete living is that kind of living which makes for direct and indirect self-preservation, proper rearing of young, proper performance of the duties of citizenship, and proper enjoyment of the leisure of life "

422.   Education: meaning of adaptation, many-sided environment, efficiency.

"Education, then, as a concrete matter becomes the shaping and guiding of the development of the child towards adaptation to and appreciation of his many-sided environment; it is an adaptation which includes the development of efficiency."—*Butler.*

(a) *Explain "adaptation," "many-sided environment," "efficiency "*

(b) *Show how the study of your specialty may con-*

*tribute to the student's education in the respects men-
tioned in the foregoing excerpts.*

ANSWER APPLIED TO LATIN, (*a*) The late Professor John Fiske pointed out the significance from
an evolutionary standpoint of the greatly prolonged
period of human infancy   He showed that just as it
was by the superior development of his brain and
mental life that man in his long race-infancy so far
outstripped his fellow creatures in the struggle for
existence, just so the human child requires a long
period of infancy to repeat the history of the race
and to become fitted to meet the conditions of modern human life, so vastly more complex than that
of any other animal.   In·the first few years the
child attains the race inheritance in his physical
life, but by far the greater part of his infancy, extending perhaps as late as his twenty-first year, is
concerned with the development of his intellectual
and moral life so that he may be able to meet all
the demands of human existence.   This is what is
meant by adaptation,—the child repeating the experience of the race, so as to become fitted to live
well the complex of the most advanced civilization

Human life is indeed very complex.   Aside from
physical development, which must always be accorded a liberal share in any scheme of education,
the race has progressed in the realm of the mental
and moral life in various ways which call for separate consideration.   We might consider the subject
under Herbert Spencer's well-known, fivefold
classification of human activities; or for the purposes of education aside from the physical, we may

well use Butler's classification of race-inheritances
to which the child is entitled. These are (1) the
scientific, (2) the literary, (3) the institutional,
(4) the aesthetic, and (5) the religious inheritances.
These five race-inheritances of Butler's together
with the physical inheritance, constitute the environment of the child in the relation to life. In
view of the above classification of inheritances and
environments of the child, the meaning of the term
"many-sided" is obvious.

Now the prolonged period of human infancy, in
which the child is to come into his race-inheritances, is a period of preparation for complete living.
Education, as has been asserted by Locke, Rousseau, Herbert Spenceer and others, and as is now
the prevailing doctrine, is not for the university,
but for life. In other words, viewing it from an
evolutionary point of view, education is to enable
the child to become successful as an individual, in
the struggle for existence, and also to take his place
and fulfill his larger duties in the social and institutional life of which he is a part. That is what is
meant by "efficiency." It is a restatement of Herbert Spencer's doctrine of complete living See
section 74.

(b) The study of Latin, while contributing to
some extent to the institutional and aesthetic inheritances of the child, derives its chief value from
its bearing on the literary inheritance. It was the
use and growth of language, perhaps, as much as
any one single part, that raised the ancestors of
man above their fellows of the brute creation.

Thought without expression perishes with the original thinker. The ability to use language clearly and forcibly in speech or writing, is a sense of power to any man of whatsoever occupation or trade.

The study of Latin can be defended mainly as it leads to efficiency in the use of English. This it does in several ways: (1) by enlarging the vocabulary through a knowledge of Latin derivation of English words; (2) by the growth of power in choice of words, one of the chief factors in good writing or speaking. This the study of Latin accomplishes by constant practice in translation, a process involving a careful analysis of thought and weighing of words, discriminating as to all their niceties and shades of meaning. (3) By acquaintance with masterpieces of structure and expression, for example, the masterful oratorical periods of Cicero, and the majestic, stately flow of the Vergilian hexameters. Such a study of Latin brings an insight into the structure and function of language much more certainly attained thus than by an exclusive attention to the mother tongue.

423.   Education.—*Name the five evidences of education enumerated by Butler.*

ANSWER.

1.   Correctness and precision in the use of the mother tongue.

2   The refined and gentle manners which are the expression of fixed habits of thought and action.

3   The power and habit of reflection by which

the mind is taught to answer questions as How? Why? through science and philosophy.

4. The power of growth.

5. The power to do —*Educational Review*, November, 1901

424. Happiness the aim of education.

The aim of education is to render the individual, as much as possible, an instrument of happiness to himself, and, next, to other beings.—*James Mill.*

Criticise this opinion.

ANSWER. "The utmost that we could expect of the educator, who is not everybody, is to contribute his part to the promotion of human happiness in the order stated. No doubt the definition goes more completely to the root of the matter than the German formula. It does not trouble itself with the harmony, the many-sidedness, the wholeness, of the individual development: it would admit these just as might be requisite for securing the final end.

"A very different aspect is that wherein the end of education is propounded as the promotion of human happiness, human virtue, human perfection. Probably the qualification will at once be conceded, that education is but one of the means, a single contributing agency to the all-including end. Nevertheless, the openings for difference of opinion as to what constitutes happiness, virtue or perfection, are very wide "

425. Meaning of education.—*Give, within a limit of three hundred words, your conception of the meaning of education.*

ANSWER   President Butler of Columbia University defines the meaning of education as a gradual adjustment to the spiritual possessions of the race. These possessions are grouped under five main divisions. A scientific inheritance, a literary inheritance, an aesthetic inheritance, an institutional inheritance and a religious inheritance.

Butler's meaning implies a threefold development of the child through his intellectual, moral and physical nature. He would have the child through self-realization possess the power and willingness to adapt himself to his environment   To do this, the child must appreciate what progress other generations have contributed to him, such progress being considered an inheritance by Butler The scientific inheritance includes a knowledge of geography, nature study, physics and mathematics; the literary inheritance includes all forms of literary composition and interpretation; the aesthetic inheritance includes drawing, music and all other kinds of art tending to form a higher conception of life; the institutional inheritance includes political geography, civics and history; and the religious inheritance includes all training tending toward spiritual perfection   Butler gives due consideration to all the activities of the mind. His meaning of education is apparently the ideal of this generation

Spencer defines education as a preparation for complete living. He would have the child possess that knowledge which is most useful   In complete living Spencer includes five activities · direct self-preservation, indirect self-preservation, the rearing

of children, social demands and citizenship, literature and art, etc. Scientifically Spencer would prepare the child for the activities of life by leading
him through the same stages of development as
those experienced by the race in its development.

Self-preservation is the constant intelligent care
of the life God has given; indirect self-preservation
is the required wage-earning to provide the necessi-
ties of life; the rearing of children includes attention
to food and clothing as well as to moral and intellectual development; social demands and citizenship imply service to society and the state; and
ability to enjoy to the fullest the leisure hours of
life can be gained through a knowledge of literature and art. Spencer makes science the base of all
knowledge and in so doing, as Butler says, deified
education.

By combining the theories of DeGarmo, Herbart,
Horne, Harris, Eliot and Maxwell with those of
Butler and Spencer, a comprehensive idea of the
meaning of education may be deduced. That education is a twofold process: the development of the
individual and his adjustment to society is the consensus of opinion among the leaders of present day
educational thought. The child must be brought
into possession of the intellectual inheritance of the
race; he must be taught to care for and develop his
body that it may be a fitting agent of his mind; his
hand should be trained to be a skillful tool; his
moral education should lead to a courageous, single-
minded devotion to duty. The individual's measure
of worth is computed in terms of service. The man,

who, through self-realization, has arrived at the fullness of his powers is measured by his efficiency in his environment Horne says education is self-realization through self-development for self-hood and social service Every educator has dwelt on either the development of the individual or his adjustment to society and many lay equal stress on both Nearly two thousand years ago this interrelation of man and society was expressed by the Great Teacher in the words, "No man liveth to himself."

426. **Same as 425.**

ANSWER   In order to form an ideal of education, we are forced back upon the experience of the past, for a basis of judgment. What shall we select out of this past experience as the fitting heritage of the individual? Butler says the individual is entitled to his "scientific, literary, aesthetic, institutional and religious inheritance." The spiritual inheritance of the race will fall under these divisions. One can imagine an individual possessing a large share of the first three, and still falling far short of the modern ideal of education. But in order really to possess his institutional and religious inheritance he must have experienced many varied relationships with his fellow men Consequently we find Dewey emphasizing "social stimulus," or the adjustment of the individual to his environment. But this environment is the product of race development in successive epochs. The child passes, in a general way, through the same stages. Consequently true education will seek to give the individual the best

products of the race at a time when his development is best suited to receive it In order, however,
to arrive at this goal, something more is required
than merely to give the child his proper mental
food. He must be enlisted in his own cause, and
must react in a healthy way upon the stimuli presented. In other words, we must arouse him to that
conscious direction of his own powers, which we
call self-activity. Then we shall get that happy harmonization of interest and effort which produces
self-realization When self-activity is once aroused
on the lines of a many-sided interest, a physical, intellectual and moral interest, we shall certainly
have a person of character and efficiency. Such a
one ought to fulfill Spencer's ideal of "complete
living" He ought to be able to efficiently provide
for his direct and indirect self-preservation; perform
his duties properly in the rearing of the young, act
the man's part in the duties of citizenship, and,
finally, be fitted for the enjoyment of a noble leisure
in the pursuit and contemplation of the aesthetic
achievement of the race.

Terms Defined

427. **Abstraction.**—*What is abstraction? Illustrate.*
Abstraction is the mental process involved in retaining the common qualities which belong to all
the individuals of a certain class and rejecting the
uncommon qualities A complete process of abstraction results in the concept or general notion.
It is synonymous with conception

428.   **Analogy.**—*Define, illustrate and criticise reasoning by analogy.*

Analogy is a kind of reasoning in which an inference is made on account of the resemblance of two things.

Illustration.   Porto Rico, a former Spanish possession, has inhabitants able to control themselves. Then the same is true of the Philippine Islands.

Criticism.   Such reasoning is not conclusive There may be many points of likeness, but one great difference can overthrow the similarities Analogy can be used only when the points of likeness are overwhelming   For application in nature study, see Dexter and Garlick, 179

429.   **Apperception.**

Apperception is mental assimilation.   It is the gaining of the understanding of new knowledge by means of past experience and knowledge   I see a strange flower.   I recognize it as a flower by means of my former knowledge of flowers I have seen

430.   **Assimilation.**—*Define assimilation as used in psychology*

ANSWER.   Assimilation is that process in consciousness by which previously united contents form new combinations by uniting with other material   It is a form of mental synthesis.   "On the nervous side it rests upon the direct coalescence of sensory processes " (James)

431.   **Circle** of thought.—*What is meant by the circle of thought, as used by the Herbartians?*

The circle of thought for any pupil is the limit of personal interest of the pupil in the subject-matter of instruction, or in matters outside of the school. It is distinctly the work of education to extend the circle of thought so that the pupil may become interested in as many lines of investigation as he is capable of carrying on without reaching the result known as smattering in education. The fivefold division of the course of study in our elementary schools illustrates a many-sided interest which should give every pupil the desired circle of thought to prepare him for future efficiency An application of extending the circle of thought is found in Lang's *Educational Creeds*, page 150: "A boy spends his play hours in fishing, catching birds or butterflies; and he is in danger that his fine feeling, sympathetic heart will harden. Would punishment direct the content of his will to nobler pursuits? Would it thoroughly cure him? Certainly not It would sooner increase the danger. The thoughtful educator pursues a different course He seeks to build up a new interest in the thought-circle of the boy. He calls his attention to the beauty of the flowers, explains to him their nature and various kinds, shows him how to raise plants and how to take care of them, how to press and dry them The probabilities are that he will spend his recreation hours in cultivating plants, in botanizing, and in making a herbarium."

432. Clearness.—*What is meant by clearness in education?*

Clearness in education is that stage of method in which the mind of the pupil apprehends the presented facts with clearness of mental vision; the first formal step in method is clearness according to Herbart.   The preparation as usually understood in the formal steps of instruction is a means to clearness.

433. Harmonious development.

Harmonious development refers to a balanced development of all human powers   This development includes mental, moral and physical training.   It is what is sometimes called a development of the whole man; and it is the kind of training that Spencer requires for complete living

434. Image.

A mental image is a revived percept   While reading the other day I came upon the name "Vineyard Haven"   At once there came to mind the picture of the Haven as I had seen it one evening at sunset, when the different crafts were anchored for the night.

435. Imitation.—*Define imitation as ordinarily used in education*

ANSWER   Imitation is the adoption by a person of a thought, a feeling, or a volition, suggested by the presence of a similar thought, feeling, or volition in his social environment   The latter may be copied either consciously or unconsciously. Consult Horne

436. Inhibition.—*Show meaning and application of inhibition in teaching.*

Inhibition means witholding or stopping any form of psychological or physical activity.   An extreme effect of fear may inhibit respiration and circulation for a moment   A child's attempt to speak on the stage may inhibit the action of the salivary glands so much that the mouth seems dry. Anger, happiness or fatigue may partially inhibit all mental activity for a short time. This application of inhibition shows the necessity of maintaining uniform working conditions in school.

Another use of inhibition comes under habitation. Suppose certain tendencies to evil are observed. Instead of trying to inhibit the tendencies by breaking off abruptly, we try to work gradually toward disuse by substituting desirable habits Thus we find the words *disuse, inhibition, substitution* and *direction* under methods of treating impulses, instincts and habits.

437.   **Learning through self-activity.**

"Learning through self-activity" means that the child shall be directed so that his own efforts may be the means of education. It involves a knowledge of what to study, how to study it, and where to find it. It presupposes attention to the directions; of the teacher and interest in the matter to be mastered Self-activity is a process tending toward self-realization; it is, in fact, the one safe way of attaining the fullness of self-development which is the aim of all education

438.   **Logical memory.**

A logical memory is a memory which reproduces to minds events or ideas through their logical connection or continuity. It differs from mere rote memory and recalls by means of association I know the date of the founding of St. Augustine. I wish to recall the date of Santa Fe. I have

learned that there are seventeen years' difference
I then compute and remember the date of Santa
Fe. This is example of logical memory.

439. **Manumental training.**—*What is the connotation of the term manumental?*

ANSWER. The term "manumental" is used in
order to emphasize the fact that the real function
of the manual training furnished by other than
special trade schools must be primarily educative.
The purpose is not merely to train the hand to
work skillfully, important as that is, but to reach
the mind through the training of the hand as an
instrument of acquisition and of expression.

The term is used here also with a wider meaning than has attached to "manual." Under it is
included all forms of school work with materials
of any kind, kindergarten occupations, drawing,
modeling, sewing, and cooking, work in wood and
mental and school gardening. "Manumental
training" means all school employments that typi-
cally represent or reproduce the material constructive and productive activities of society.—Roark,
Economy in Ed., p. 177.

440. **Many-sided interest.**

The aim of instruction, therefore, is not the production of a many-sided knowledge but of a
many-sided interest. (Rein.)

*Explain this statement, and give reasons for accepting
or rejecting it*

ANSWER This statement means that if we have
a many-sided interest we have a full development
of all the powers of the mind and many-sided

knowledge will result. Life is a process of learning from beginning to end. We do not stop learning when we leave school. If our powers for learning have been cultivated interest will lead to the
necessary knowledge. While if the aim has been
for many-sided knowledge we may both lack the
knowledge and the power for gaining it. If this
meaning is accepted I accept the statement in the
above.

441. Mental discipline.

Discipline is that training of a faculty which
gives it power to accomplish more than it would
have been able to accomplish without such discipline So mental discipline means a training of
the mind, with a view to accomplishment as expressed in the definition.

442. Method-whole.

A method-whole is an outline or plan of a certain amount of subject-matter which can be considered as a unit. The method-whole has been defined as an arrangement of matter that may be
presented according to inductive-deductive method It has been explained as a process of passing
from particular notion to general notion. A
method-whole may embody all of the work presented during a month, as the drainage of New
York State Then that larger method-whole may
be sub-divided into other method-wholes, according to the work of a week or a day. Thus the
definition of an adverb is suitable for a method-
whole; but in that work there is another method-
whole embodying the lesson on the verb. In short

it is an arrangement of subject-matter to suit the natural capacities of the class.

443. **Reaction.**—*What is meant by reaction in psychology?*

ANSWER. Regular response to stimulation is reaction. Education as a process consists in furnishing proper stimulation and in directing the responses.

Sensuous impressions are not properly educative if they fail to beget a correlative motor activity. The physiological process is this: (1) impulse from external stimulus is transmitted through sense organ to nerve centre; (2) the translation in the central process; (3) the changed impulse is transmitted to the motor organ. "Every idea tends to realize itself in action." In teaching it is necessary, therefore, to see that there is a reaction; that the impression receive its complimentary expression through verbal reproduction, written reproduction or material reproduction as exemplified in the various forms of manual training.

444. **Self-realization explained.**

Self-realization may be defined as consciousness or harmonious development In order to arrive at this goal, we must emphasize the two great principles of education, apperception and self-activity. In dealing with apperception we shall be obliged to consider the individual or subject of apperception; and the subject-matter to be apperceived The study of the individual will lead us to the consideration of many useful physiological laws, such

as the doctrine of interest, the place of effort, the
necessity of proceeding from the particular to the
general, the culture epoch, and we shall thus work
in harmony with the nature of the mind. The
consideration of the subject-matter of instruction
will help us to avoid one-sidedness In order to
attain true development all the powers of the
mind must be exercised We must, therefore, provide a curriculum rich in scientific, literary, aes-
theic, institutional and religious instruction.

But we must never forget that these provisions
will all be of no avail unless we secure the self-
activity of the subject of our education. We can
lead a horse to water, but we cannot make him
drink, however good our intention, however fine
the water, if he have no thirst. The interest of the
pupil must be aroused in order to realize that
happy relation between teacher and pupil, in which
the activity of both is directed toward the same
end.

445. Sensation.

A sensation is a simple mental state resulting
from a physical stimulus. While at work this afternoon, I became conscious of a noise outside. I
paid no attention to it until some one inquired if
we kept pigeons. We found later that some children were drawing a box along the sidewalk at
some distance from the house. The first state of
mind in which a noise was heard but its nature or
cause unknown, was sensation.

446. Socialization.

"The immediate aim of the school should be expressed as socialization."

Interpret and apply this expression of aim.

ANSWER.   The socialization of the individual requires, in addition to the maximum development of the physical and mental powers, the highest possible development of social good will, social intelligence and social habits   The development of social good will and social intelligence implies . a curriculum consciously adapted to that purpose. The approach toward an ideal curriculum involves an increasing demand upon the material of the social sciences   As to the formation of social habits, it implies the organization of the school so as to provide the greatest possible number of opportunities for social action.—Basic Ideas of a Scientific Pedagogy by J. W. Howerth, Ph.D., of Chicago University, in *Education,* November, 1902, p 137.

447. Social stimulus.—*Explain meaning and application of social stimulus.*

Persons or ideas are called sociable if they are in harmony. Sociable means agreeable. Transfer the idea of a sociable company of workers to the school, and there apply the thought of (a) good will, (b) mutual agreement, (c) working   There is a stimulus under such conditions. It does not come wholly from the teacher, nor from any one pupil; each pupil is contributing something. The stimulus coming from the members of a society or group or society is social stimulus. The social stimulus is a good working spirit in a school; it is good public opinion among the pupils; it is community interest rather than selfish individual interest.

448. Suggestion.—*Define and illustrate suggestion as used in education.*

Suggestion is the tendency of consciousness to believe in and act on any given idea.—Horne, *Principles of Ed*, 284.

Suggestion is useful with pupils in all cases where the act does not demand the time and the power of personal reflection by the pupil. The pupil may be thinking well up to a certain point, but there he hesitates A word, a sentence, a look or a gesture from the teacher may be enough to help him continue the train of thought. Thus in grammar, a pupil may have completed all the analysis and parsing excepting one word in a sentence He has said that word is an attribute complement but he fails to decide the part of speech. The teacher asks what parts of speech may be used as an attribute complement; the pupil names the three and then selects the right one.

The teacher's glance at a boy's shoes may be suggestion enough for next morning, pointing to his own head may suggest the use of comb and brush; the teacher's appearance is a powerful suggestion, the teacher's penmanship, blackboard work, conversation, personality,—all work strongly by suggestion. This shows the relation between suggestion and imitation, law of association, etc

449 Syllogism.—The syllogism is a form of de-

ductive reasoning in which a conclusion is drawn
from two known premises

Major premise.   Human beings are rational.

Minor premise.   You are a human being.

Conclusion.   Therefore you are rational.

450.   "Things before words."

"Things before words" is a concise way of
expressing the aim of realism.   In the sixteenth
century there was a movement against Latin and
Greek and in favor of French and German, geography, science and other real things.   It was argued
that the study of Latin and Greek was largely
a matter of memorizing forms   The aim of the
realists, therefore, was to put pupils into touch
with their environment   Another meaning of this
expression is seen in the inductive method.   It is a
process of learning by experiment instead of by
reading or listening.   Pupils handle natural things
and use their own self-activity; they get a knowledge of the real things, their properties, their uses,
etc., before the principle or rule is put into words.

451.   Visualization

Visualization is mental imaging as a means of
reproducing visual experiences   The earlier stages
in the process consist of presenting objects for
study; directing attention to what is desired, and
otherwise training the power of observation, re-
moving objects and then drilling in the formation
of images.   A second phase in the process is objective, i e., illustrative, presentation of lessons
This means the use of objects for illustration rather
than for showing the characteristics of the objects

themselves   The third contribution to the process includes all other graphic methods, such as drawings, writings, charts, maps, pictures, etc

One practical illustration of training in visualization is the practice of teaching memory selections, declensions, classifications, or other matter, from written forms upon the blackboard   This plan invites comfortable posture of pupils and teacher; class attention, interest, and concentrated effort, social feeling and consequent social stimulus, the application of the law of contiguity; and, as a result, commendable self-activity and desirable habits of study.

452. **Culture, instruction, induction, culture epoch theory, humanism, scholasticism.**—*Explain the meaning of each of the following terms: culture, instruction, induction, "culture epoch theory," humanism, scholasticism.*

ANSWER.   For   definition   of   culture,   see *Epitome*, page 2.   A satisfactory explanation is quoted from the *Dictionary of Philosophy*: "Culture refers to the comprehensive changes in individual and social life, due to the continued and systematic influences of mental improvement and refinement. Considered from a strictly sociological point of view, it is called civilization, but anthropologists make culture the broader term   In the individual it is Education.

"Whatever affects the intellectual status of man, whether directly or indirectly, may be said to be an element in culture.   Arts and sciences, language and literature, education and government, social customs, ethics and religion, contribute directly to the culture of a people, but practical industries, means of transportation and communication, and the physical comforts of life exercise, particularly in modern times, no less profound, though more indirect, an influence upon the totality of human culture"

2. Instruction. See Chapter X. For another answer, take the next two paragraphs from *Dictionary of Philosophy*:

"Instruction is the teaching act whereby the pupil is informed and also trained and stimulated to acquire knowledge and mental power.

"It concerns itself chiefly with three things: the materials, the course, and the methods of instruction"

3. Induction. See *Methods in Education*, p 91.

4 Culture epoch theory. See Section 99

5. Humanism was an educational movement which sought to secure the refining influences from the subject-matter. Classical Latin and classical Greek were used as the principal sources. The derivation of the word humanism suggests its meaning, namely, to humanize, civilize, give culture.

6. Scholasticism was an educational movement to reconcile philosophy and Christian doctrines. It existed from the ninth to the fifteenth centuries, reaching its climax in the eleventh and twelfth. Abelard, a Benedictine, was the greatest teacher, Thomas Aquinas (1225-1274), a Dominican, known as the Angelic Doctor, was the greatest writer,

Duns Scotus (1265-1308), a Franciscan, was another noted writer. The schoolmen used the lecture method, interpreting and commenting upon the subject matter; and also the syllogism which is a form of deductive reasoning in which a conclusion is drawn from two known premises

453. Motive, instinct, intuition, breaking the will, suggestion.—*Explain and illustrate the following terms. Motive, instinct, inhibition, "breaking the will," suggestion (as used in psychology).*

1. Motive is any conscious element considered as entering into the determination of a volition — *Dictionary of Philosophy.*

2. Instinct See chapter VII

3. Inhibition is interference with the normal result of a nervous excitement by an opposing force.

It differs from paralysis, in case of which the nervous action is prevented, while in case of inhibition it is overcome, diverted, or neutralized. The normal effect of a higher upon a lower center of a series is the partial inhibition of the lower. Reflexes may be inhibited voluntarily or by the strong stimulation of sensory nerves up to a certain point

Physiologically, inhibition is a necessary condition in preserving the balance and tone of bodily function. The ganglion cells of the heart, for example, are constantly inhibited by the vagus nerve, and similar control is exercised over all other vital processes. As James says, "we should all be cataleptics and never stop a muscular contraction once begun, were it not that other processes simultaneously going on inhibit the contraction. Inhibition is therefore not an occasional accident; it is an essential and unremitting element in our cerebral life." The exact nature of the process remains obscure.—*Dictionary of Philosophy*

4 "Breaking the will" means forcing the child to do what the parent or the teacher wishes, irrespective of the wishes of the child. See 469 for quotation on balky will In that connection James says Such children are usually treated as sinful, and are punished; or else the teacher puts his or her will against the child's will, considering that the latter must be "broken." "Break your child's will, in order that it may not perish," wrote John Wesley. "Break it as soon as it can speak plainly—or even before it can speak at all It should be forced to do as it is told, even if you have to whip it ten times running. Break its will, in order that its soul may live." Such will-breaking is always a scene with a great deal of nervous wear and tear on both sides, a bad state of feeling left behind it, and the victory not always with the would-be will-breaker.—*Talks to Teachers*, p. 182

5. Suggestion includes the instigating factors or phenomena in the social environment which leads to the adoption, by a person, of a thought, a feeling, or a volition, either originally or for the time being absent from his consciousness.—Geo. B. Germann, *Teachers' Monographs*. April, 1901, p 52.

Suggestion is the tendency of consciousness to believe in and act on any given idea.—Horne, *Principles of Education*, 284.

Suggestion is useful with pupils in all cases where the act does not demand the time and the power of personal reflection by the pupil.

An indirect suggestion is that which furnishes a motive for the pupil's act without commanding the problems of the thing. A positive suggestion secures the right act in the right way, while a negative suggestion amounts to prohibition. Forbid the evil as little as possible, fill consciousness with the good as much as possible.

Dr. Quackenbos has treated deficient pupils by post-hypnotic suggestions, but such methods cannot be generally commended. Such a method has been used for the purpose of building up the nervous system enough to promote self-control in those cases where self-control is really desired. Only a deficient person is a subject for hypnotic treatment by suggestion. In the valid use of suggestion with normal persons the line should be drawn exactly at that point where the individuality of the person is no longer his own but has become anothers.—Horne, *Principles of Education*, p. 290.

For further study, see James, Principles of Psychology, Chapter XXVII. Stout, Manual of Psychology, 269 to 275 Stratton, Experimental Psychology and Culture, Chapter XI. Dill Psychology of Advertising, page 4 Mason, Hypnotism and Suggestion, Chapter IV supra.

Priciples Applied

454. **Attention.**—*Define, discuss and illustrate attention.*

(a) Attention is concentrated consciousness
Hume says attention is consciousness occupying
itself with an object. In consciousness we are aware
of many thoughts and objects, but in attention all
the powers of the mind are directed to one thing
or object. In the best forms of attention an object
or sound may be directly presented to the senses
and yet I am unaware of the fact. We give best
attention when there are no physical or psychical
obstacles. For instance, I am very tired, bodily
tired I go upon a street car Usually I attend to
things going on around me. Now, I give no attention to them. I am too conscious of my weariness.
This weariness is a physical obstacle which inhibits
attention to the things around me.

I pick up a book in Russian. I open it and I try
to interpret it. I fail. I lose interest and find my-
self unable to conscentrate my mind upon the book
It is too difficult for my mind I have no apper-
ceiving-group to bring the power upon an object
Therefore, I cannot give attention because this is
a psychical obstacle

Attention is of two kinds, voluntary and involuntary I am attending a course of lectures There
are no physical obstacles in the way of my attending, that is, I am not tired The room is warm
enough, the air is good, and all other physical environments are satisfactory There are no psychical obstacles The speaker's topic may be new to
me, but it is not beyond my comprehension. The
speaker begins and I listen and follow the trend of
his thought. I am giving voluntary attention.

The speaker occupies a position on a small stage To the left is a door partly open About the middle of the lecture a small dog peers in the doorway and runs across the stage to someone he knows in the room By an involuntary act my mind leaves the trend of the lecturer's thought for a few minutes and pays attention to the dog This is involuntary attention. So involuntary attention is consciousness, not controlled by the will, occupying itself with an object Voluntary attention is consciousness controlled by the will, occupying itself with an object

(b) A voluntary action is an action performed as the result of a volition on the part of the doer. It implies that the doer knew what he was doing and he did it of his own free will It also implies that the action was performed as the result of the interpretation of vibrations by the brain rather than the result of an interpretation in a nerve center located outside of the brain in the spinal column.

Illustration. I am working at my desk The window is open. The wind blows a sheet of paper against my hand. I remove the paper without being conscious of my action and without taking my thought from the work in which I am engaged. This is an involuntary action A few minutes later, during the same kind of study, I hear of a friend's illness. I stop my work and immediately prepare to go to see that friend. I am conscious of what I am doing, but I do it of my own will This action is voluntary action.

455. Attention.—*What is attention? Is the distinc-*

*tion between voluntary and reflex attention ultimate?
Discuss. What is meant by expectant attention? Ex-
emplify some of its effects and give what you consider
to be their psychological explanation.*

ANSWER. Attention is focussed consciousness.
A single object or idea holds the central point in
consciousness, other objects and ideas making up
the "fringe of consciousness." The effort required
in answering this question pushes aside all other
contending elements. Attention is not a mental
process but a condition necessary to get the best
mental results. It implies adjustment of sense organ, of one's whole physical and mental make-up.
In thinking out a problem, there must be a certain
facial expression, a posture of body, a tension of
nerve and muscle, etc., if the end is to be attained.

Reflex or involuntary attention precedes voluntary
attention in the individual's life-time. In the lower
forms of animal life and in primitive man every act
of attention was accompanied by movement, e. g.,
every act of attention was reflex. While no apparent movement results in a case of voluntary attention, there is movement, nevertheless, which manifests itself in the changed bodily process. The
simplest thought affects the flow of blood. So that
ultimately, voluntary and reflex attention are the
same. As reflex, automatic, instructive, random,
impulsive and sensory movements must precede
voluntary movements, so reflex acts of attention
must precede voluntary acts of attention.

In *expectant attention* there is the mental preparation, the adjustment of the sense organ as well as

the adjustment of the entire nervous system, to receive the stimulus. This state makes the reception
of stimuli more rapid, more impressive and more
accurate. In the class room, expectant attention
may be aroused by a look, a pause, a question, by
an experiment, a suggestion, etc. Expectant attention places the emphasis on the motor expression
resulting from stimuli rather than the reception
of stimuli. This sometimes leads to hallucinations,
to too great susceptibility to suggestion, and to the
giving of wrong reports. Both the advantages and
disadvantages of expectant attention should be attributed to the motor expression of sensory impressions.

456. **Interest and activity.**—*Show the relation of
interest to activity in education.*

ANSWER. The doctrine that the interest naturally attaching to the ends for which pupils should
be awakened in the means (i. e the studies) used
for reaching them; and, conversely, that permanent
interest in the ends should be fostered through the
means

When interest attaches to the end, but not to the
means for reaching it, we have drudgery, as in the
case of a workman who thinks only of the dollar,
taking no pride or interest in the labor that earns
it; on the other hand, when there is interest in the
means but none in the end, we have play, not
work. Interest is then only amusement When,
however, there is interest in the end to be attained
by activity, and also in the means for reaching the
end, we have the type of work desirable in educa-

tion. A direct interest, therefore, should be aroused in the studies as the means of reaching the ends of education; this interest when thoroughly aroused has a reflex influence in developing true ideals of life and conduct. The mental attitude of the sculptor is the ideal one for the pupil, since the interest he feels in the statue as an end attaches to every stage of its creation. When this direct interest is moral as well as intellectual and aesthetic, then instruction becomes truly educative —DeGarmo in *Dictionary of Philosophy.*

457. **Interest: native to acquired; importance.**— *Illustrate the fact that acquired interest grows out of instinctive or native interest.* (18)

(b) *Show the importance of interest in mental life.* (8)

ANSWER. (a) To the average man a specimen belonging to the order of Coleoptera—or for that matter to any other order of insects—and so minute as to be incapable of examination by the naked eye, could not be called an object of more than passing interest Yet a friend of mine, a young naturalist of no mean attainment, could study that little insect for hours and find it a positive pleasure. This young entomologist, whom I have known from boyhood, is to me a living illustration of the passing of native into acquired interests, and of the importance of interest in mental life.

Born and reared on a large farm, he knew no other books and teachers than the domestic animals and fowls, the fields, the woods, and the brooks, life, motion, sound and color, the things natively

interesting to children. While yet a mere boy, the
fishpole and the gun furnished him with the health-
iest of activities, trained eye and ear, and schooled
him in natural cunning and shrewdness better than
a thousand stories of Jason or Achilles. Next came
the collecting impulse. He acquired a practical
knowledge of taxidermy, and the birds of the field
and the forest fell to his gun, not out of wanton
cruelty, but for a real purpose—to form his collection. Already his native interests were passing into
a higher stage. It was now not alone the flight,
color or striking appearance of the bird that at-
tracted him; it was also knowledge about the bird
which was being unconsciously added to its naturally interesting features.

When he moved into town to get a high school
education, he not only possessed a collection of
finely prepared bird-skins, as well as one of insects
of all kinds the locality afforded, but he had mastered the rudiments of scientific classification, and
no thanks to teachers or tedious lessons. Through
these four years of high school training, the algebra
and Latin grammar had their place, of course; but
he still ranged the country with shot-gun and in-
sect-net, and his collections grew in size as well as
in skill of preparation and arrangement.

Though he had not especially distinguished himself in text-book knowledge during his preparatory
course, when he entered college there was a sudden
ripening of the funds of long years of preparation—
a marked man in Natural History from the day of
his entrance; and before graduation he was an as-

sistant in his special department. In every subject
he touched, he attained distinction, and when he
left the university to obtain a professorship elsewhere, he had made one of the best records in general scholarship ever attained in that institution.
And what was the secret? There had been no
forcing, no compulsion, no rebellion against dry
lessons and dull teachers. He had builded the whole
super-structure of his education on the simple native interest of his boyhood activities, without a
struggle and almost without effort. Observation,
discrimination and judgment—the essentials of
scholarship—had been trained not in the hothouse
of the school, but in the woods and fields and under
the open sky. This is an education "according to
nature."

(b) The foregoing sketch shows better than any
long expositions the importance of interest for
mental life. It is the link between the mind and
object or idea. It is the basis of involuntary attention, from which all voluntary attention must proceed. It is the gate to apperception, through which
the new idea must pass before it can be introduced
to old and related ideas. It is the lubricant which
keeps the machinery of education running smoothly
without friction or squeaking. It is the arch-
enemy to dullness and stupidity on the part of
both teacher and pupil; to disorder by the latter
and crankiness by the former. It is the pillar that
supports the temple of education. It is the death
of mediocrity and the key to scholarship.

458. Interest and literature.—*Define interest in*

the educational sense   How may interest in literature, or in history, or in botany, be cultivated and made permanent?

ANSWER.   Interest, in the educational sense, implies a liking for the different subjects in the school curriculum.   Upon the awakening of interest depend not only the results a pupil reaches in a subject, the attitude toward the teacher and the school, but also the probability that he will continue any of these studies when he passes out of school   Again, the interest pupils have in school work determines, to a large extent, the number of years they are willing to spend in school.   Interest, to a large extent, is a safe index by which the quality of teaching may be judged   Where interest pervades the work of the school, discipline is secondary.   But interest is not the only end to be kept in view.   Application, review and drill, also, have their place.

To create an interest in literature the pupil must first be impressed by the enthusiasm of the teacher. Such enthusiasm affects all the members of the class   The selections the teacher reads to this pupils and the selections read in class must be adapted to the age and developments of the pupils in the class   Selections they can supplement and interpret by their own experience arouse interest   Selections that offer ample opportunities for the exercise of the imagination delight pupils.   Selections that are units of their kind appeal to children.   At times, the teacher should read just far enough to arouse the interest of pupils to a high degree.   Let them look up and complete the reading of the selection. The teacher should interest pupils in library books by selecting, now and then, books which she knows will appeal to particular individuals. In this way the love of literature is made permanent.

459. Apperception.—(a) *Define apperception.* (b) *State and illustrate a principle regarding its application in the teaching of your specialty.*

ANSWER. Applied to Latin. (a) Apperception is the process by which the mind assimilates new ideas to its fund of related ideas.

(b) The idea to be apperceived must not be new or strange; or, to put it in other words, the mind must be prepared to receive the new idea, by having at hand an apperceptive mass of related ideas ready to seize upon the first one. For instance, the subject of noun-declension strikes many a beginner in Latin as something entirely new and strange. When he is first directed to learn the paradigm of the first declension, and in perhaps the very next section of his book to translate case-forms of other nouns, he often feels that he is trying to solve a Chinese puzzle.

Now the duty of the teacher is clear. In a very few words he can call up before the mind of the pupil the fact of declension in English grammar, surviving in the pronoun, and he can impress on them the fact that the change in ending accompanies, or rather indicates, a change in relation. Then passing to the noun, the teacher should point out the possessive case still surviving and may tell the class that the English language once had other cases but has lost them, and now indicates the meaning of the noun largely by its position in the sentence. He can show them how Latin, possessing a complete case system, admits of a freer order and indicates the relation of the noun by the case-ending.

Further, if the book does not give with the Latin paradigms and meanings a parallel table of English cases,—e. g , Genitive *linguae*, (a) (the) language's or of (a) (the) language, English possessive or objective with "of," let the teacher elicit from the pupils such a table, by their giving the English cases corresponding to the several translations. This table of English cases should be learned as thoroughly as the paradigm and translations, all this preparation being given the class in the recitation before they are set to work learning their paradigm. Besides this, the teacher should show the class how to decline any other first declension noun by finding its base, adding the same table of endings, and using the same form for translating Again, before the pupil is plunged into an exercise of translating case forms of various nouns, he should be shown that he should continue first the number, then the case of the noun. When all this preparation has been given, the pupil is ready to master the declension and translate the exercises, feeling that there is just enough new to interest him and stimulate his effort

460. **Apperception, failure in.**—(*a*) *State three causes of failure to apperceive.* (*b*) *How or why does the correlation of studies aid apperception?*

ANSWER. Since apperception is "the process of unifying and making 'meaningful' the data furnished by sensation," it involves three factors. These are: (1) perfect sense-organs to receive the stimuli which occasion sensations; (2) attention, the condition through which the sense-organs are adjusted to suit the stimulus to the best advantage; (3) the number of related ideas present in the mind to interpret the new experience. If any one of these elements is defective or wanting altogether, the apperceptive process is weakened. Suppose that one's eye-sight is defective, it is difficult to interpret visual stimuli. When the child does not pay attention to the lesson, he neither sees nor hears what's going on. If you never studied algebra, you can't interpret algebraic symbols.

In the correlation of studies the teacher does not make use of material taken from two or more studies in order to teach more or less of all of them but he uses the material the child has learned in another subject if the use of that material serves best to give clearness to the lesson taught. Thus, one teaches the geographical position of two armies if, by doing so, the history lesson can be made clearer by doing so. In this way correlation becomes an indispensable aid to the process of apperception.

461. Apperception and memory.—*Tell, with reasons, what memory has to do with apperception, and what apperception has to do with memory.*

ANSWER. To understand clearly the relation existing between memory and apperception it is

necessary to define our terms. In memory acts
we recall the ideas of former experiences and recognize them as having been in our consciousness
before, as when a person remembers an impressive
conversation he had with another person In apperception acts the mind interprets new experiences
in the knowledge of old related ideas To the illiterate the written sentence, "Dare to be true," means
nothing. To the child its meaning is very hazy.
To the mature individual who realizes its many-
sided significance it means much There may be
memory without having any apperception as is the
case where a former experience is exactly recalled
in detail. If, however, a new element appears in
the reproduction we have apperception. But apperception means primarily that the mind contributes as much of old experiences as it can to explain
the new. To make this possible old experiences
must be remembered, i e , without memory there
could be no APPERCEPTION, no such mental contribution Apperception is, therefore, a law of memory Without apperception there could be no
percepts of anything since every percept is made
up of the two elements, sensation and apperception If there were no percepts there could be no
memory of any. Suppose that you don't know a
word of Greek, a Greek sentence is given you for
translation. Why can't you translate it? Why
can't you remember it? Apperception is wanting.
There is no percept of it, in consequence Hence,
there can be no memory of it

462. **Feeling and intellect.**—(*a*) *Trace the con-*

*nection between feeling and intellect; between feeling
and will or action. State educational corollaries and illustrate their application.*

ANSWER. Feelings are bodily states. Intellect is
purely a mental process or a certain number of mental processes. If the bodily manifestations of feeling, such as the brightness of the eyes, the faster
circulation of the blood, deep inhalations and ex-
halations of breath, the beaming countenance, are
suppressed, feeling disappears. Feeling, or interest, in a thing determines to a large extent what
we shall know about it. The condition and circumstances of a very deserving person are brought
to your attention. Now, you know his needs. You
feel sympathy for him. If your act is completed
you take steps to help him. The latter is an exercise of will.

Corollaries to be drawn from these facts are: (1)
Inform the mind as to what is right and proper;
(2) Evoke the feelings toward worthy ends; (3)
Make many occasions for pupils to exercise their
feelings in attaining these ends.

Let us suppose that the expression, "pleasurable
excitement," is not due to the gratification of a
purely selfish motive. Spencer evidently means
that the activity the individual engages in becomes
a means through which the individual expresses his
own spontaneous activity. The solving of problems in arithmetic is as eagerly done as the playing
of a favorite game. If this be true the individual
will get the greatest amount of culture out of it.

463. **Principles underlying habits.**—*Name two*

principles underlying the formation of habits. Illustrate the application of each of these principles.

Two principles underlying the formation of habits are plasticity and regularity of repetition. Habit is a fixed tendency to act, feel, or think in a certain way under certain conditions. In order to form a fixed tendency, we must give this fixed tendency exercise by repeating again and again and yet again that thought, act or feeling we wish to become a fixed tendency. I wish to wean children from the incorrect pen holding habit to the correct. My first lesson teaches the children how to hold pen My second how to hold pen and use pen in that position Each following lesson it is my duty to see that child always holds pen correctly. If this is done, in time there will be a fixed tendency to hold the pen correctly If my lessons are a week apart I find the hand forgets its tendency more readily than if I had my lessons every day I find five minutes each day devoted to writing forms better writers than twenty-five minutes a week in one lesson devoted to subject. Then I conclude it is better to have frequent regular short intervals than regular long intervals.

464. **Actions: reflex, instinctive, voluntary.**— *Distinguish reflex, automatic, instinctive and voluntary actions. Under what conditions do voluntary acts tend to become relatively unconscious? Can this fact be explained by any general laws of nervous action?*

ANSWER Reflex actions are those actions which do not require consciousness for their performance. They are performed by the spinal cord and the lower centers of the brain. As examples, may be mentioned the winking of the eyelids, the dilation of the pupil, the clutching and the sucking reflexes, etc. In physiological terms, the simple reflex is the action of one or more sensory neurones upon one or more motor neurones in the lower centers of the central nervous system.

Automatic actions are to be distinguished from reflex actions on account of their more complex nature. They do not require consciousness but require the connections of many more sensory and motor neurones. Besides, some automatic actions involve the sympathetic nervous system in addition to the lower centers of the central nervous system. Among automatic actions may be mentioned the heart-beat, movements of the digestive organs, movements required in breathing. Some psychologists call those actions automatic which no longer require conscious effort to be performed. The former definition is generally accepted, however.

Instinctive acts are the results of a pre-determined setting of the entire nervous system to reach in a certain way. These acts are the results of racial experiences. Like reflexes they are purposive. They help to protect the life of the individual, in certain instances. For example, one finds himself in a very dangerous physical position, as in the way of a train. There is no time for decision. Instinct helps us to get out of the way, we wonder how. Instinctive acts are to be distinguished from reflexes and automatic actions in that their occurrence is known to consciousness.

Voluntary acts require consciousness before and after their occurrence. They require conscious effort They are based directly on the co-ordination of the movements which took place as results of reflexes, automatic adjustments, instructive and imitative movements, random movements and movements due to sense stimulation. If these latter movements had never taken place one would have no memory of their occurrence and their repetition would be impossible just as I can't remember an experience that never took place. When voluntary acts have been repeated until the nerve-chain becomes well united and more easily stimu-, lated than any other, the execution of the movement begun is transferred from the conscious cerebral region to a lower brain center. The movement begun remains seemingly unconscious unless the chain is interrupted by something very unusual As examples, piano playing and performing the routine of one's life may be mentioned.

465. Action: reflex, impulsive, automatic, deliberate.—*Define and illustrate each*

Reflex action is the process of changing an afferent nerve current into an efferent nerve current without the aid of the brain

Illustration I put my finger on a warm object; the afferent nerve carries the message to the nerve center, where the efferent nerve receives the return message to remove the finger. This action takes place without the aid of the brain and is thus called reflex action

Impulsive action is that in which the entrance of

an idea into consciousness is immediately followed by the appropriate action. As an illustration, suppose I am hurrying to the post office to mail a letter. While on the car I see a friend from a distant city. I run at once to greet him. This is impulsive action.

Automatic action is habitual action. Any action becomes automatic as soon as it is carried on without any intervention of the will. An illustration of this is the finger action in playing a piano after a person has become accustomed to that kind of action.

Deliberate action is that in which (1) action is suggested to the mind (2) the mind considers whether it will act or not, and (3) the will makes the decision. This is illustrated in the decision of many teachers who begin to consider the advisability of teaching in New York City, think of the matter a year or two, and then decide for or against the action. This process is sometimes called deliberation.

466. Active, mobile children.

"Some children are more active, or mobile—more suggestible; while others are more passive or receptive, less suggestible. The impulsive, active children are always responsive, but always are in error in what they say and do; they are quick to generalize, poor at making distinctions and they are characterized by fluidity of attention. The sensory or passive children are more troubled with physical inertia, more conteemplative, less active in learn-

ing to act out new movements, less quick at taking a hint, etc " (After Baldwin.)

*Comment on this classification.   Suggest ways of
dealing with each of these types.*

ANSWER   I do not agree that impulsive, active
children are always in error in what they say and
do, are quick to generalize, poor in making distinctions and characterized by fluidity of attention.
This designates some impulsive, active children,
but not all   I have one in my school at present
who could be so characterized   This one can naturally see just why I have had her repeat the work
of last year.   Last year she gained absolutely
nothing.   This year I hope to have her gain sufficient to be promoted in June .   With the second
characterization of passive children I agree.   I
have had until just now such a boy in my school.
He likewise is repeating last year's work   His
physical inertia is so great that I could not hope
to have him up to grade by June.   He has therefore been removed to a special school where individual attention can be given in hope of bringing him to grade.

467.   Correlation.—*What is correlation?*

ANSWER.—Correlation is the result of Herbart's
education through instruction   It means arrangement of the program so that the work in one subject may, as far as possible, throw light on the work
the pupil is doing at the same time in another work;
and (2) such a method of teaching as will cause
the pupil to see the particular fact he is studying in

relation to all that he knows.—Gordy, *A Broader El. Ed.*, p. 194.

468. Correlation, variety, induction, miscellaneous or simultaneous questioning, concrete methods. —*State (do not merely refer to) educational principles upon which each of the following methods or devices may be defended:—*

(*a*) *Uniting in one lesson history and geography.*

(*b*) *Having a lesson in arithmetic (grammar grade) followed by one in music or in reading.*

(*c*) *Presenting or having the children present a number of sentences, each containing a pronoun and its antecedent, before formulating the grammatical rule about the agreement of the pronoun with its antecedent.*

(*d*) *Teaching by giving questions to the class and requiring answers from one or more individuals designated after each question is put.*

(*e*) *Choosing the object rather than a picture of the object in a nature study lesson.*

ANSWER.—(a) The principle of correlation is founded upon the law of association of ideas and apperception; briefly stated, it is that quality of the human mind which makes it easier to keep a fact in a group of kindred related facts than to hold it as an isolated idea. Correlation usually refers to association between groups as, the Delaware is a river in N. J. (geography); Washington crossed the Delaware (history). To have both these facts at the same time helps the memory.

(b) Voluntary attention develops out of involuntary attention. In small children the capacity to attend to one subject is limited to a few moments.

If pursued longer fatigue is experienced. Therefore variety in the program of studies is a psychological necessity. The principle is, therefore, variety.

(c) The human mind is of such a nature that it is obliged to proceed from the "known to the related unknown." Principle: induction.

(d) Clear localization in consciousness is the first great necessity of securing memory. If the question is put after the child's name is called, this localization of attention is often missed. Instead of getting the question in mind, the child thinks, "Oh, I'm not the one this time." Simultaneous questions preferred.

(e) The principle of "multiple sense impression" insists that an idea is best held in consciousness. when it is carried over as many roads as possible. To touch, handle, taste, smell and see an object will be four times as useful to the memory of it as it would be to simply see it. Concrete methods require the thing itself whenever possible.

469. Will: James on balky will.

"The teacher often is confronted in the school-room with an abnormal type of will, which we may call the balky will. Certain children, if they do not succeed in doing a thing immediately, remain completely inhibited in regard to it; it becomes literally impossible for them to understand it if it be an intellectual problem, or to do it if it be an outward operation, as long as this particular inhibited condition lasts."—James.

(a) *Describe wrong ways of dealing with such cases, with their usual or natural results.*

(b) *Describe a psychologically right way of dealing with such cases. Give reasons.*

(a) This quotation from James is found on page ·8⁻ in *Talks to Teachers.* "Such children," he says, "are usually treated as sinful, and are punished; or else the teacher puts his or her will against the child's will, considering that the latter must be broken. Such will-breaking is always a scene attended with a great deal of nervous wear and tear on both sides, a bad state of feeling left behind it, and the victory not always with the would-be will-breaker.

(b) The answer is quoted from James. "When a situation of the kind is once fairly developed, and the child is all tense and excited inwardly, nineteen times out of twenty it is best for the teacher to ap-perceive the case as one of neural pathology rather than as one of moral culpability. So long as the inhibiting sense of impossibility remains in the child's mind, he will continue unable to get beyond the obstacle. The aim of the teacher should then be to make him simply forget. Drop the subject for the time, divert the mind to something else; then, leading the pupil back by some circuitous line of association, spring it on him again before he has time to recognize it, and as likely as not he will go over it now without any difficulty."

470. **Will: method of training.**—*Outline a useful method of training the will.*

One means of training the will is that of allowing as much liberty as possible to the individual pupil, to throw him upon his own resource and responsibility; giving him certain work to be performed within a specified time, leaving the exact time, place, and manner of doing the work to him. Allow him the freedom of the room, the building, the grounds, with the understanding that the privilege must be rightly used. The point is to get him in the habit of acting on his own initiative and to exercise proper control over his actions; both important functions of the will.

Suggest to pupils various things that they might do to improve their village or to alleviate the distress or add to the happiness of people less fortunate than themselves. Arouse their feelings to the point where they are ready to *do* something, then put the opportunity before them.

Organize little clubs or societies for the accomplishment of certain special ends, as the protection of the birds, the cultivation of a flower garden. Furnish all the needed instructions as to how to do and create the desire to do, but leave the *doing* to the children.

Faculties

471. Sensation: defined; distinguished from perception.—*Define sensation Explain its relation to perception. Give a full account of its distinguishable characters.*

ANSWER.—A sensation is the simplest mental process resulting from bodily processes connected with definite bodily sense organs The first stimulation of a special or organic sense organ, whose effect resulted in the first consciousness of the child, produced a pure sensation. As soon as the memory

of former experiences aids in the interpretation of
the effect of new stimuli, or new sensations, we
have perception. Now, sensation is no longer pure
as a mental content but the mental content is made
up of sensation, the direct result of stimulation, and
apperception, or the mind's contribution to the
effect of the present stimulus. These two elements
—the sensation element and the apperceptional element—together make up the percept. The mental
process involved in arriving at the percept is known
as perception. Every percept must include these
two elements. So long as this is the case the mind
gets. new mental material. The mental material remains static or decreases when no new sensations
are experienced. Sensations have four attributes:
quality, quantity. intensity, and duration. Their
quality is determined by the sense-organ whose
stimulation gives rise to them. The quality of smell.
sensations differs from those of sound, sight. taste,
pressure, etc. The quantity of sensation element
depends on the amount of sense-organ surface stimulated. The intensity of sensations depends upon
the manner in which the stimulus is applied, e. g.,
the plain sensation may be increased by an increase
of physical pressure. The duration of sensation depends upon the length of time the stimulus is applied; as, the prolonging of a musical tone.

472. **Imagination.**—*Define, classify, and apply.*

ANSWER.—Imagination is the power of thinking
or calling into consciousness feelings of things, persons, qualities and conditions of all sorts not present

to the senses. It is twofold in its nature, productive and reproductive.

In its reproductive nature, it corresponds to the various senses. It is, for instance, possible to divide images into audile, visual, gustatory, motor and tactile images. Some people are stronger along one line of image-making, some along other lines. The attempt has been made to classify people according to their type in this respect. The teacher there talks to the audiles, writes on the board for the visual, makes motions and enunciates prominently for the motors. As it cannot, however, be proved that the people who see images most clearly before their mind's eye necessarily make the best responses, and as all children possess these powers in some degree, such attempts seem questionable. Thinking is forever aided by getting images of things to be stored away in memory as clearly as possible because vividness is one of the factors in memory.

In its productive power, imagination has resulted in the best achievements of the race. Imagination, in this direction, is the power to put parts of things, qualities, and conditions into new forms. We call this creative imagination. This functions largely in ethical thinking or idealization. Here we get a construction of all the qualities which appeal to us as standing for the highest good.

The uses of the imagination may, therefore, be classed under two heads, (a) its memory uses (b) its creative uses.

The abuses of the imagination may be thought

of as (a) failure to get clear images or failure in visualization, making for weak memory; (b) over-emphasis of images rather than responses, benumbing to self-activity.

The creative uses of the imagination may be thwarted by crushing out individuality, telling too much in history; talking too much in drawing; failure to direct thought toward original thinking.

473. **Image: defined, applied.**—*What is a mental image? Describe two kinds of imagination. Show by illustrations from literature, geography and mathematics how the imagination may be trained in school.*

ANSWER.—A mental image is the memory of a revived percept. This morning you sat at your breakfast table. Now you picture to yourself the scene there. You see the other members of the family at the table. You see the arrangement and color of dishes. You know the courses in their order. You taste the deliciousness of the things you had to eat. You smell their fragrance. You can hear what was spoken while you sat there. You can feel how you felt as you sat there. One, several, or all of these elements may enter into your mental image.

The mental products of imagination may be possible of realization or not. If they are, we have constructive imagination. If they are not, we have fancy or phantasy. In either case the elements combined are not new. They must have been experienced. Imagine an electric railway built from New York to Chicago. The elements are not new. The product is possible of realization. Hence this

is an instance of constructive imagination. Imagine
an electric railway built to the moon. The elements
are old. The product is not possible of realization;
phantasy. The inventor works out a product which
will be useful to mankind in a material way. The
poet writes of things beautiful and good. Both use
constructive imagination.. Both kinds of constructive imagination are possible of realization. Both
benefit mankind.

In literature the imagination is trained if the
writer does not do the work for the reader by de-
scribing every detail of the scene. Swift's *Gulliver's
Travels* is a good example.

In geography the student, by means of the imagination, can comprehend the meaning of a moun-
tain if he knows what a hill is. He can imagine an
ocean if he knows what a bay is or what a lake is.

In mathematics he can solve his problems to better advantage if he can project the theorem so that
is dealing with real angles, or if he thinks he is
actually selling in the market place.

474. Imitation in children.—*Discuss the imitative-
ness of children of four to six years of age, in its relation to their development.*

ANSWER.—Of all animals, the man animal is the
most imitative. The first acts which the child of
the kindergarten age does are those due to instinct.
These are imitations of the acts of his ancestors.
Among them are the desire for play, for freedom,
for examining strange things, etc. Through the
gratification of these desires he develops physically
and gains knowledge of his environment. He imi-

tates those with whom he is thrown in contact consciously and unconsciously. The language he hears becomes his language the countenance he sees modifies his countenance. Manner of walking, sitting, standing, etc.,—all become a part of his acquired experience. All of these acts are steps in the gradual adjustment to environment. The models he imitates serve either as a check to his development or as an aid to it. Instructive imitations, imitations of the simple and the complex acts of others, help to give physical and mental determination to the child's development. A further recognition of this fact implies that the power of imitation is continuously operative until the individual has reached his complete development. Not only this, but one generation advances beyond that of its predecessor by imitating its successors and shunning its failures. See Horne, *Philosophy of Ed.*, pp. 175-187.

475. **Impression and recollection.**—*Name four of the most important conditions which tend to fix an idea in the mind and to render it easy of recollection. (b) Explain the terms used in answering (a). (c) Illustrate the use of one of these conditions in teaching.*

ANSWER.—(a) Impressions are made on the central nervous system through the various sense-organs. The impressions which one receives through handling an apple, seeing it, tasting it, smelling it, hearing it fall, taken together constitute the percept of apple. The memory of this percept is the idea. To make this idea most permanent it is necessary (1) that the same impressions should be often repeated, (2) that they should be recent,

(3) that they should be received with the best attention, (4) that they should be received through the greatest possible number of sense-organs, i. e., they should be received with the greatest possible number of associations. (b) Adhering to our example, this means that to remember apple, the individual must (1) taste, smell, handle, hear and see it often, (2) that he must recently have done so, (3) that not one or two but all sense-organs possible be involved, (4) that the taste, smell, sound, sight, feeling, of the apple be attended to when received, (c) in teaching the causes of the French and Indian wars this would mean that the lesson must have been taught recently, that teacher and pupils gave it their undivided attention, that the lesson has been often reviewed, that the lesson was taught in its widest historical and geographical relation. The preceding attitude of the French and English toward one another, the purpose of their settlements, the nature and place of their settlments, the attitude of the Indians in these struggles, the possible chances of success, etc., all enter into the full significance of the lesson.

476. **Memory: repetition.**—*"Repetition is the prime influence in memory."*

"Of two men with the same outward experiences the one who thinks over his experiences most, and weaves them into the most systematic relations with each other, will be the one with the best memory."

(a) *Show wherein, if at all, these quotations are consistent with each other. Give reasons. (b) Explain the meaning of the second quotation. (c) Give three practical reasons as to the most effective way of committing to memory a specified poem.*

Answer Applied to English.

(a) "Repetitio mater studiorum" is an old maxim in education; and too often the repetition was of a mere mechanical nature,—simply going over again the facts to be learned without throwing any new lights upon them or attempting to bring them into any systematic relation. In this way, the catechism, multiplication table, and a large amount of historical data were hammered into the minds of children for generations. This form of repetition as an aid to the memory depends upon the law of contiguity, viz.: that objects or ideas occuring together in time or space tend to recall each other.

The second quotation is not entirely consistent with the first, for repetition is not limited to one process. There is the mere mechanical repetition already discussed, but there is also another kind, repetition by the association of ideas. Both forms of repetition are important aids to the memory. Both may be exercised upon the same facts or ideas. Therefore the quotations are consistent. The second form, however, is much more valuable as it develops the powers of discrimination and judgment and leads to logical memory.

(b) The second form of repetition depends on association by similarity or contrast. Here the chances of recall are greatly multiplied by the idea being interwoven into systematic relations with other ideas of the same sort. This kind of repetition is practically the same thing as the association of ideas, which constitutes the basis for apperception. Two men might read the same passage from a historical work an equal number of times, and one see merely a succession of historical events. The other, looking to the law of cause and effect and noting relations of similarity and contrast, not only sees the inner meaning of what he has read, but can recall the several facts with little effort, because they are woven into a logical fabric by the threads of association. His mind is like the telephone system of a large city. He can give every incoming idea a "connection" with almost every other he possesses.

(c) 1. Study the life and character of the author, the events of the time and the influence that called the poem forth, and, as far as possible, try to breathe the same atmosphere and feel the same feelings that prompted the poet to the creation of his work. 2. Read the whole poem over several times; first as you would read any piece of literature, getting the spirit and idea of the poem as a whole; the second time analyzing the poem into parts and getting a clear perception of the meaning of each part; the third time, fixing the attention on the relation of the parts to each other and to the whole poem. 3. Make a special study of all allusions, new words and words used in special senses, and the thought echoes from one part of the poem to another. Then memorize not by mechanical repetition of words, but by linking all the parts into a chain of ideas, and thinking this

chain through, until the movement of the thought
is perfectly familiar, and the whole poem becomes
a part of you as truly as it was a part of the author.

477. Serviceable memory.—*What are the characteristics of a serviceable memory? How far and by what
means may it be cultivated?*

Memory has three stages:
1. Apprehension or fixing in memory.
2. Reflection or keeping in memory.
3. Reproduction or bringing to consciousness
    when needed.

In order that a memory may be serviceable. attention must be paid to all three stages. Each is
of importance.

Apprehension is of great importance. Sense impression is its fundamental law. The stronger the
impression made upon the senses the greater will
be the power of retention and reproduction.

If the first stage has been well begun, retention,
or keeping in memory is not likely to be a difficult
action, i. e., the thing fixed is not likely to sink so
far into sub-consciousness as to be impossible of recall. The third stage presents repetition or reproduction as a necessary adjunct of a serviceable
memory. As the race loses power of any faculty
which remains unused, so the mind forgets the
thing fixed and held in memory if that thing is not
called to consciousness for use at various intervals.
For instance, I once fixed or impressed in memory
a certain Latin word. Memory held that word in
subconsciousness ready for use. I neglected to

bring to consciousness after a certain number of repetitions. I now have forgotten the word

A serviceable memory, then, is a memory which responds to the needs of normal conditions of life. Such a memory requires exercise and plenty of it All the work of school and life tends to cultivate memory

478. Association of ideas.—*State or describe the doctrine of association of ideas, and illustrate by showing the applications of it in the learning of history*

ANSWER. The doctrine of association of ideas, simply stated, means that if two associated ideas enter the mind, the recalling of one of those ideas tends to recall the other   These conditions give rise to two fundamental laws of association,—Association by Contiguity and Association by Similarity   Titchener has reduced these to one law, that of Association by Similarity. The law stated in physiological terms is, "That any two ideas which have one or more elements (neurones) in common tend to recall one another upon the consciousness of either " When you learned that Columbus discovered America, you also learned the date, 1492. The date is not remembered by reason of its resemblance to Columbus but by reason of the fact that the impression was received contiguously at the same time or in immediate succession.   The two impressions stimulated the same area on the brain   Those brain connections are still strong enough for one idea, Columbus, to call up another, 1492. But when Columbus suggests John Cabot the fact of simultaneous impression is quite likely totally absent. The name Columbus recalls the name Cabot because *several common elements (neurones) are involved*, such as, their native country, both being sailors, both being sent out on a similar mission, etc. In the former example one idea recalled another because the impressions had been received simultaneously or in immediate succession. Here the force of association is due to actual common brain neurones involved.

479. Abstraction.—*What is abstraction? Illustrate.*

ANSWER. Abstraction is the mental process involved in retaining the common qualities which belong to all the individuals of a certain class and rejecting the uncommon qualities. A complete process of abstraction results in the concept or general notion. It is synonymous with conception.

In arriving at the concept, adverb, I abstract the definition that an adverb is a word that modifies a verb, adjective or another adverb by noticing that it performs those three · functions. The spelling, length, and form of the word are not found common in all adverbs and so cannot be taken as parts of the definition of an adverb.

480. Concept, conception, particular notion, general notion.—*Define and illustrate each.*

ANSWER. A concept is the mental content corresponding to a general name. The concept is the tag we put on particular things to put them into their proper classification. For examples, This is a man, This is coal, etc. Man and coal are the general terms standing for concepts.

The mental process involved in arriving at the

mental content, concept, is conception. It is the mental process involved in thinking individuals into their proper classes.

A particular notion is the idea one gets of an object through one sense alone, or through several, or through all the senses. Thus, one may get a particular notion of a chair through the sense of sight alone, but he gets a more complete particular notion, or percept, of the chair through sight and touch. The latter meaning is usually inferred.

A general notion is the mental content corresponding to a general name. It differs from concept in that it has reference also to the persisting common qualities in individual living things. Thus, the general notion of a certain person whom you know enables you to label and know him as that particular person regardless of the physical, mental and moral changes he may undergo. The general notion is synonymous with concept when it stands for any class name, as: noun, man, page.

481. Concept: formation; imperfect explained.— *(a) What are the stages or steps in the formation of a concept? (b.) Mention four causes of imperfection in concepts?*

Concept is the name given to a general idea, such as apple, man, tree. Take for example, the development of the concept, "man." Under the first step, presentation of material, the greatest possible variety of specimens of human beings, is considered. These are compared with one another, their common characteristics retained and the uncommon ones rejected. Under this head there would be ruled out such diverse characteristics as color of hair, color of skin, size, speech, etc. When the common qualities are retained and the concept is classified, we say (1) that man is a thing having physical existence, (2) he is a living thing, (3) he is the reasoning living thing. Hence, our definition says, "Man is an animal that reasons." Every concept implies species, genus and differentia.

The four causes of imperfect concepts are: (1) the examination of an insufficient number of various individuals belonging to the same class; (2) inaccurate use of terms by which we seek to define qualities of things, (3) imperfect percepts of the material presented, (4) inaccurate abstraction due to loose grouping of what are supposed to be common qualities which distinguish one class from all others.

482. General notions.

"General principles (concepts, laws) without particulars are empty; particulars (percepts, facts) without general notions are blind."

Explain this principle Illustrate its application.

ANSWER. In a complete process of apperception were found the two processes, induction and deduction. To arrive at the concept or the rule we had to have a sufficiently varied number of individual cases. These were compared and associated. The quality, or qualities, common to all was retained and the definition formed. Where these steps are not employed in arriving at the rule, the rule is empty and meaningless. To tell pupils that to add fractions you must make the denominators common is a general principle but empty in itself. Having given the rule in this way the pupil sees no essential relation between the rule and the individual cases falling under the rule. Suppose that all the. experiences the individual has in his life-time remained separate things, that no unification or grouping into classes was possible. There would have to be a name for every human experience. The experiences of different individuals to which we give a common name could not even be grouped Each individual would have his own name for every percept he had as a result of every new experience. This being the case, language would be impossible. Mere percepts would be blind. It takes individual percepts to give meaning to concepts and concepts must be had to see percepts   For example, the pupil must first learn what a name is by examining many names of things. After he knows that a' name is a name he can recognize names as names and not before this.

483.   Mind-wandering. — (a) *Describe mind-wandering, and give the psychological causes of it.*

b) How can mind-wandering be overcome.or cured?

No matter how scatter-brained the type of a man's succesive fields of consciousness may be, if he really care for a subject, he will return to it incessantly from his incessant wanderings, and first and last do more with it, and get more results from it, than another person whose attention may be more continuous during a given interval, but whose passion for the subject is of a more languid and less permanent sort. Some of the most efficient workers

I know are of the ultra-scatter-brained type. One friend, who does a prodigious quantity of work, has in fact confessed to me that, if he wants to get ideas on any subject, he sits down to work at something else, his best results coming through his mind-wanderings. This is perhaps an epigrammatic exaggeration on his part; but I seriously think that no one of us need be too much distressed at his own shortcomings in this regard. Our mind may enjoy but little comfort, may be restless and feel confused; but it may be extremely efficient all the same.— James, *Talks to Teachers*, 114.

484. Mind-wandering.—(*a*) *Describe mind-wandering, and give the psychological causes of it.* (*b*) *How can mind-wandering be overcome or cured?*

ANSWER. When a mature individual can not keep his attention focused on one idea or thing for any length of time, he is said to be affected with mind-wandering. Since this is the natural state of children's attention we do not, in that instance, speak of mind-wandering.

Mind-wandering may be due to an undeveloped voluntary attention or it may be due to the contention of ideas which appeal to the individual's mind with equal force.

The cure for the former kind of mind-wandering is found in applying one's self to report a certain experience accurately. The account should be short but emphasis must be laid on its accuracy. Having accomplished this end, report accurately a more complex experience, etc. As an illustration, let the subject accurately report the contents of a single sentence, then, of a paragraph, then of a page, etc.

The second kind of mind-wandering, James thinks, needs no cure. The fact is, that by means of such mind-wandering the individual often happens upon the very point he could not arrive at in any other way. For example, the solution of a problem is not possible for the time being. Another line of activity is taken up All at once, the problem appears in a new light and is solved.

485. Judgment and conception. — *Distinguish between judgment and conception, and show the close connection between these two processes. What is meant by saying that "all our judgments are at first synthetic, though they tend to become analytic as our knowledge of things is perfected?"*

ANSWER. Conception is the mental process by which a general idea is reached This general idea is given a name, such as: book, dog, etc. Through judgment we compare two concepts, noting their agreement or disagreement. For illustration, let us take the sentence, "Man is an animal." The two concepts compared here are man and animal. In determining whether a thing belongs to the class animal, in noting every quality judgment must be passed whether that quality would admit the possibility of its being placed in that class. The same is true in arriving at a proper classification of individuals embraced by the term MAN. In deciding whether four-footedness is a characteristic necessary to decide whether a thing belongs to the class animal or not we compare the concept "four-footedness" with "animal " In our decision we make a judgment. Conception and judgment are mutually dependent. We must have concepts to be compared to have judgment and we must have judgments to arrive at a concept.

"Judgments are at first synthetic, though they tend to become analytic as our knowledge of things is perfected," means that we first "generalize and then analyze." A child sees a rhinoceros for the first time. At once, he calls the animal a cow, the thing which it most nearly resembles. The judgment is synthetic. A closer study of the rhinoceros by which the child corroborates his synthetic judgment or refutes it by getting a closer knowledge of the thing is analytic. The same would be true of the statement that the child has never seen an animal like it. Closer study reveals whether his statement were true or not. The fact remains that the first judgment is synthetic and closer study of the thing requires analytic judgments.

Conduct of the Recitation

486. Heuristic method.—*What is the value of the heuristic or laboratory method?*

ANSWER. The heuristic method tells the pupil but little directly; it leads him on by questions and problems. It avoids the leading character of the questions of the Socratic method, but aims to put the pupil into the attitude of a discoverer by proposing questions and problems whose replies are not obvious though within the power of the pupil. This method is essentially active and constructive.— Young, *The Teaching of Mathematics*, p. 61.

487. Induction, deduction. — *Distinguish between induction and deduction in teaching and state your views as to the appropriate uses of each.*

Induction is a process of reasoning which establishes a general rule, definition or principle from the knowledge of particular cases. I wish to teach that a noun is a word used as a name. I write five sentences containing nouns. I question. How is such a word used? It is the name of ——. I continue until all nouns have been so treated. Children give words used as names. At end of lesson tell children what words used as names are called. Children learn definition A noun is a word used as a name. This is the process of teaching noun by induction.

Deduction is the process of reasoning by giving a general rule, definition or principle and applying it to particular cases.

I give the definition. A noun is a word used as a name Children learn. I write five sentences on blackboard. Children find words used as names and call them nouns? This is teaching noun by process of deduction.

Induction is the process of finding out principles for one's self. It is experimental. It is speculative. Deduction is the process of taking opinions of others and verifying or applying those opinions.

Both kinds of reasoning are useful. Every well taught lesson should embrace both. Children should be taught by inductive-deductive process wherever possible. That is, teacher should be questioning, etc , elicit general rule from children and then give them plenty of opportunities to apply their own rules. The first part is inductive; the second, deductive.

488. Assignment of lessons criticised.—(*a*) *Criticise each of the following ways of assigning advanced lessons, and in each case suggest a proper assignment:* (1) (*In history*) *Study all about the first voyage of Columbus and be ready to tell me what difficulties he met in getting aid, and everything of that kind." (2) (In civics) "Find out as much as you can from your parents, or from any other source, about the Government of the City of New York." (3) (In science or nature study) "Take for to-morrow the next....pages." (b) State with principles founded upon your reasons, three principles to guide in the assignment of lessons.*

(a) (1) Careless work on the part of the teacher. Enough work is suggested to the earnest student to discourage him. The average student needs a more direct assignment with reference to certain places for it.

Suggested assignment: Why Columbus wished to find a route to India. His plan to reach the Indies. Reason for this plan. How viewed by the people. Efforts to secure aid. Result. First voyage. Equipment. Starting place. Incidents on voyage. Land! Character of natives.

I would not assign more than the topics preceding the "First Voyage" for one lesson.

(2) Wrong, for most people know very little of the way a city is governed. It is a general question not likely to interest pupils or engage the attention of the pupil's parent. Some parents would probably give undesirable information.

Suggested assignment: Ask pupils to find out at home, if no books are available, who arranges for the lighting of the city every night, and who pay for the care of the lights. Or, how are school buildings secured! How are the principals and teachers paid?

Either of these subjects would represent something touching the child's life; hence, better subjects.

(3) Very bad. To assign so much work from a book when so much material is at hand is inexcusable. Memory will be trained, but imagination, reasoning and judgment are higher powers and more delightful ones to engage. Suggestion: We are to talk about the dragon-fly to-morrow, and I wish you to be able to tell then where the dragon-fly is often seen and why he likes such places. Why is he one of our best insect friends?

(b) Following are the principles to guide in the assignment of lessons:

(1) The ability of the pupil.—It is useless to ask a child to do more than he is able.

(2) The time at his disposal.—A high school teacher made the remark that she expected the pupils to work at least one hour on her subject. When asked what the pupil would do if each teacher required the same amount of time, replied that she had not thought of it in that way.

(3) The ground to be covered.—In our school system a certain amount of work must be done each year. To accomplish this a teacher must assign enough work each day to cover the ground.

489. Discussion in class.—*Treat the subject of discussion as an element in class instruction under the following heads: (a) Advantages of discussion in class. (2) (b) Dangers in such discussion. (3) (c) Directions for creating and profitably conducting a discussion. (3) (d) Characteristics of effective discussion. (5) (e) Illustrations of profitable discussion in class, showing mode of creating and guiding it. (5)*

Answer. An accepted answer is given in full in outline form in *Methods in Education*, p. 95. Put that matter into essay form if you prefer the essay form.

490. Education outside of class instruction.—*Describe the ways in which a high school teacher can subserve the educative ends of the schools through activities not directly connected with the scheduled class instruction. (15)*

Answer. A high school teacher, especially one regularly in charge of a classroom, can in many ways besides class instruction subserve the educational ends of the school. First of all, there is the matter of regularity and promptness in attendance. By carefully investigating cases of absence and tardiness, he can help the student to form the habits of regularity and promptness so truly essential to success. Again, the general attitude of the pupil toward the school and toward his studies is a matter in which the teacher can make himself an influence. A boy may be obstreperous or disagreeable in the recitation of some particular teacher; and, in such cases, the teacher in general charge of the boy can co-operate with the teacher of the subject, to the benefit of all parties concerned. Further, the use of time, especially before school in the morning, is an important point to the student and the teacher in charge of the room should see to it that every individual boy uses his time to the best advantage

In short, the teacher must consider and become familiar with the individuality of all his students, so that he can be sympathetic in all his relations to them. The fact that the teacher shows an interest in other subjects besides his own, and sometimes gives helpful suggestions in regard to lessons in those subjects, goes a long way toward making him respected by the boys. Further, the record of all his class in their various subjects should be scrutinized by the "official class teacher" so that he can discover the boy's trouble and help him where he can.

There are other activities,—athletics, musical clubs, school papers, debating societies and the like where the teacher can and ought to interest himself, so far as consistent with his own time and strength In a large city, it is impracticable for a teacher to get acquainted with his pupils in their homes, but he should welcome every occasion of meeting their parents and friends, who sometimes visit the school, and showing that his interest in the boys is genuine A mandatory regulation in New York City (1911) provides for assignment for systematic visitation of the pupils' homes.

For further consideration of this important topic, see *affiliated interests, educational agencies,* and *supplementary activities* in index of *Methods in Education, Answers in School Management,* or this book.

491. Note books.—*What are the chief uses of note books by the pupils?*

ANSWER. The chief uses of note books are: (1) for reference work in class; (2) to record developments made in class and not found in the text; (3) to record the assignment.

When matters are being developed orally in the class the attention should not be distracted by taking notes; after the topic is somewhat formulated it may be briefly recorded as far as necessary to supplement the text. Unless fixed by notes the material is likely to be lost.—Young, *The Teaching of Mathematics*, p. 147.

Young's opinion seems to favor the study of what is printed instead of copying it. Copying as a learning process has been abused. The modern view may be summarized.

1. Use note books for research work, such as collateral reading. This permits originality.

2. Use note books to supplement text-books in regular use.

3. Use note books to record or classify essentials of daily study and recitations.

492. Too much written work.—*There is a feeling that too much written work is called for in our schools. Give three valid objections that are made.*

ANSWER. 1. It is a device for occupying the time of pupils for the sake of giving release to the teacher.

2. The papers are not criticised and returned to pupils and so it is a waste of energy.

3. The habits of carelessness and inaccuracy are

a result of number 1. Pupils know that their work is not examined and they are satisfied to submit written productions that are far below the standard of oral exercises in that same class. Much of the experience in later life depends upon the power of oral communication of thought. So much written work is not a guarantee that the pupil will be able to do what is required from him in the line of oral communication.

The positive view of the value of written work is well expressed by Young, page 147:

"The value of written exercises is evident as giving the teacher an opportunity to see to what extent the pupil has the work in hand, and what points are still weak; of training the pupil to quiet thinking, accurate work, clearness of style, orderly arrangement, to neatness, to careful expression. But the written exercises must be so conducted as to *attain* these needs. Almost all of them are often missed by an assignment too large for the allotted time."

493. **Marking pupils' papers.**—*In marking pupils' papers do you indicate what is right or what is wrong? Why? Do you use per cents or letters? Why?*

The purpose of all marking, like Socratic questioning, is twofold. The first aim is to show the child the existence of error in his answers; and the second aim to cause him, through his own efforts, to reach the truth. So the ultimate process requires the pupil to separate what is right from what is wrong—a matter of subtraction; and the teacher's plan of marking should be whatever is most helpful in causing the individual pupil or the class to attain the desired ends. Various plans may be justified.

1. Sometimes indicate both wrong and right. The child then contrasts amount correctly done with amount incorrectly done.

2. Sometimes mark only wrong. If children are becoming too self-satisfied, too easily pleased with a poorly learned lesson, arouse the instinct of pugnacity by showing him his poor work. He will strive to overcome weaknesses. See Talks to Teachers, p. 54.

3. Sometimes mark only what is right. This gives encouragement to the backward pupil and will often bring up a pupil who is laboring under discouragement. This is a good method to try with the dull, backward child of little brain but great industry. Such types are found in every school. They are the ones whom a little praise does not spoil. Tactful praise of this kind, i. e., the bringing out of good points, may also be means of converting the bad boy into the model pupil.

I should use per cent whenever the work can easily be thus marked as in spelling and written arithmetic. It is an honest way and children can compute their own marks. They like to do this. This is a good place to use emulation. Children compare per cents from week to week and try to do better.

In such studies as grammar, history, geography, oral arithmetic, etc., it is better to use letters. One cannot determine accurately the per cent in such studies as one has no exact standard of measurement. The mind gives judgment or decision in such studies as excellent, good, fair, unsatisfactory, poor. Letters may be used signifying this classification.

494. Cramming.

"Cramming seeks to stamp things in by intense application immediately before the ordeal. But a thing thus learned can form but few associations. On the other hand, the same thing recurring on different days, in different contexts, read, recited on, referred to again and again, related to other things and reviewed, gets well wrought into the mental structure" (James).

(a) State two principles of mental activity that are implied in this passage. (b) State two general rules of method suggested by this passage. Illustrate their application.

ANSWER. The college student who does not get his lessons day by day by studying each lesson carefully before going to class and, in addition, relating what he learns in class to what he first got out of the lesson, but puts off the getting of the term's work up to two weeks before the examination and then sets about to pass the final tests by burning the midnight oil for the rest of the term, "crams." By such short, constant, persistent repetition of the material covered during the term, he may be able to pass the examination but forgets nearly all he remembered up to the time of the emergency just as soon as the emergency is over. Why does he retain just so long and then forget? Why does the student who pursues the opposite course retain?

The two principles underlying these mental phenomena are, (1) that the frequency of impressions insures their retention for a short time by reason of the deepening of a single nerve pathway, (2) that experiences gradually woven into the general growth and development of mental experiences are permanently retained. The former impressions are merely stamped on the outside and soon disappear. The latter remain as a part of the thing in which they are included.

The rules of method to be deduced are these: (1) Have pupils learn by repetition things which, though not understood now, will be valuable later on when they are able to relate them to many other facts and experiences; (2) Repeat such facts and experiences, as have been learned and understood, by means of the widest possible association until they become permanently fixed. For example, under one, commit to memory literary gems for future use. Under two, after a theorem in geometry, a rule in arithmetic, a rule in grammar, etc., has been understood, commit it to memory by a sufficient number of repetitions.

495. Study, art of: three directions.—*Concerning the art of study, give three directions such as high school pupils might profitably follow. Give a reason for each direction.* (15)

ANSWER. (1) *On independence in study.* One of the chief evils existing among high school pupils is the lack of mental independence. Sometimes it takes the vicious form of copying, as in algebra or Latin composition; sometimes, as in Greek or Latin, the use of printed translations; and, again, sometimes the trouble is due to oral help from other pupils or even from the teacher. Here is one field in which the teacher can make himself a force,—in the destroying of this helpless dependence and the building up of a spirit of honest individual effort.

The teacher must take pains to ascertain the cause of the boy's trouble. Sometimes the boy does not know *where* to find out the needed information. Here is where he needs practical help in the use of dictionaries, encyclopaedias and reference works and very often, he needs help in methods of using his own text-books. For instance, many Latin students do not know how to utilize all the helps contained in their edition of Caesar or Cicero. Again, it is often defective observation that is the cause of the student's trouble, and too often it is the absence of ambition and a healthy "fighting spirit." The strenuous life has its place in school, also, and unless the boys of this age are willing to grapple with the knotty problems of their studies, it is hardly probable that they will succeed when it comes to facing the battle of life. The efficient teacher will seek to discover the cause of dependence in the individual pupil, and having correctly diagnosed the case, apply the indicated remedy.

(2) *On the making of notes.* One boy sits merely "poring over" his book, and another with pencil always in hand, jots down on paper or in a notebook the facts and points he considers important. Other

things being equal, it is an easy guess which of the two is going to make the better student. Let the student learn to take notes systematically and study always with pencil in hand. It takes more time, perhaps, and requires more effort at first, but it is an important aid to concentration, and that is one of its chief advantages. Another is that the boy is not only multiplying his impressions and consequently his chances of recalling, but he is also translating his impression into expression in terms of his own thought. He is learning discrimination between the important and unimportant. He is economizing time and learning to study systematically. Practice will enable him to tell better what is worth noting down, and what is to be passed over, and he feels that he is gaining in power, and so he is spurred on to the attaining of excellence in all his work.

(3) *On daily reviews.* The president of one of our leading universities, when advising a class of freshmen on methods of study, urged it upon them to make it a practice to review carefully each day's lesson as soon as possible after the recitation, at all events before beginning the preparation of the next day's lesson. This is in full accord with the psychology of memory and the doctrine of apperception. Not only does this daily review "fix" the recitation by simply repeating the process, but it throws new lights upon the various points and brings them into systematic relation. The student not only clears up his difficulties, but when he leaves the lesson, he leaves it in terms of his own

individuality; and if he keeps up this practice consistently, the whole work of the term is related and bound together, and the practice of cramming for examinations may be entirely dispensed with.

496. Home study.—*Outline or otherwise present your opinion on the assignment of work to be done at the homes of pupils.*

ANSWER. A paragraph on home lessons as a means of harmonization and also an outline for discussion are given on page 64 of *Methods in Education*. Another presentation is given in the next two paragraphs.

In regard to outside study, there should be no lessons to be learned at home before the twelfth year; then only three-quarters of an hour of home study. In the thirteenth year an hour may be allowed, and after that an increasing amount up to two hours. Study should be mostly done at the school under the teacher's supervision. Recitation should be short and intense, so that there may be concentration. Not more than ten or fifteen minutes in the first two years of school life; fifteen to twenty minutes the next two years; twenty to twenty-five minutes the fourth and fifth years; forty to forty-five minutes in the high school.

The arrangement of studies should be such that those requiring more mental power, more reasoning, as mathematics, science, grammar, are taken up in the morning; and but one short, difficult lesson after the noon-day recess. The line of mental energy for the day can be represented by a double curve starting at 9 o'clock, rising until 10, and then descending rapidly until 12:30, the other part of the curve starting at 12:30, rising until 2. but not to the level of 10 o'clock, and then falling with great rapidity until 4 o'clock. Music, drawing, writing, gymnastics should be used to relieve the more exacting lessons. The afternoon should be spent in manual training, games, cross-country walks, and excursions to some historical spot or museum. Every pupil should be required to get out into the air, away from his books The studious child needs this the most of all.—Dr LaFetra, of Teachers' College, in article in *New York Times*

497. Same as 496.

ANSWER Home study appears necessary on account of the stupendous task of giving to the individual any real command of his "spiritual inheritance." The amount of ground to be covered is so tremendous, the requirements of higher institutions so pressing, the examination system so exacting, that it is not within the realm of possibility to do all we are at present obliged to do in the school. It may be that our knowledge of the human mind and the possibilities of correlations are the underlying sources of the difficulty Aside from all this, however, it is advisable to assign home study for the sake of the development of self-activity and independent work so desirable in the individual.

In the last few weeks I have, however, made a successful experiment in lessening home study I believe that girls often pour over their books too long from pure conscientiousness. I suggested to some five girls who averaged in the 90's on successive tests to leave the books in my subject in the schoolroom on Friday nights. I told them I should like to see what they could do without preparation on Monday morning. I then arranged to make Friday a kind of review day as far as the recitation was concerned. I sent a number of the most backward pupils to the board with questions written on slips of paper to bring out "mooted points," did individual work with a few others, and allowed my stars to work on Monday's lesson which naturally had been assigned at the beginning of the period. The experiment has worked beautifully. Everybody wants to get into the star group and leave books in their desks Friday night. Attention has increased, and the tone of the work is good.

To summarize the bad side of assignment of lessons I should say:

(a) Attention to verbal presentation is often weak, because the child thinks, "Oh, it's all in the book anyway," which results in

(b) Consequent waste of time.

(c) Neglect of these opportunities for learning of practical matters which the home affords.

(d) Danger of new study.

498. Discovery vs. being told.—It is better for a child to discover than to be told.

(a) *Give two reasons (drawn from psychology) for the truth of this statement. (b) Illustrate a possible exception.*

ANSWER. (a) Self-activity and interest are the

two psychological reasons for the above statement. By self-activity is meant that form of self-direction which finds its primal impulse within itself. Every normal child is full of physical and mental action. If we can simply surround him with proper stimuli, his powers will develop largely without further trouble on our part. Applying this fact to education, we find experimentally that there is no real development without a great deal of this enlisted activity on the part of the child. We cannot arouse it, however, unless we secure his interest. By interest, in the psychological sense, we mean the "feeling side of apperception." In other words, he must feel that he wants to know or to do what we are trying to teach him to do. Spencer says let the child face the difficulty before the solution is presented. He will then be interested in the solution.

(b) The exception to this rule is also found in the nature of the child's mind. The power of attention in young children is limited in time to a few moments. If the child is allowed to puzzle over a difficulty too long, discouragement sets in, and interest is destroyed. For instance, if the meaning of a German sentence is not discovered, because of a forgotten idiom, there are two reasons why it is often best to tell it at once. It might incur too serious a loss of time to send the child to a large dictionary and even if this were not the case, it might divert his interest from some more important line of work, as the enjoyment of metrical form of rhythm.

499. **Concert recitation.**—(a) *From the psychological point of view what advantage and what disadvantage is there in rote or concert recitation?* (b) *To what extent and in what subjects would you make use of such an exercise? Give reasons.*

ANSWER   (a) Rote or concert recitations are usually used as memory drills. They presuppose that the thing reproduced has been apprehended and kept in memory   Now we give exercise to the third stage of every complete act of memory or the stage of bringing to memory or reproduction.   If concert recitation is used as memory drill in this manner it is perfectly legitimate as the words given by children correspond to ideas already in child's mind   Where such work is used to fix ideas for first time in child's mind it is wholly at fault psychologically.   It is in opposition to the principle that the mind should gain through the senses its knowledge of everything external to itself.   The words said do not correspond to concepts in child's mind.

(b) I should use concert work where I wished for repetition for the purpose of exercising memory and yet had not time to give each child·an opportunity to recite   Herbart recommends repetition of this kind.   It is well to use concert work also for variety   Child grows tired of always doing things in same way.   If we are sure the ideas are behind the words, it promotes self-activity   It is well to use it to overcome diffidence on part of child.   In reading for expression I find that children will imitate good expression if allowed to give in concert where a failure would result if the same recitation must be given alone.   In reading Shakspere I have been led to find where diffidence was first conquered in concert work.   Concert is useful in promoting self-activity and strengthening memory in the recitation of memory gems.   Concert recitation likewise gives social stimulus.   Children like to work together in this way.

500.   Adolescence: characteristics, tendencies, principles for guidance.

"Adolescence is the Elizabethan period of human existence.   Rousseau likens it to the Renaissance."

What characteristics of adolescence are there implied? Mention three tendencies of adolescence that may become morbidly prominent.   Give three principles to guide the teacher in the wise management of a class of adolescents.

Note.—The completed quotation reads: "Rousseau likens it to the Renaissance—the first birth being that of the body, the second birth that of the soul, the personality."   From an article on Adolescence, by Dr. LaFetra, *Teachers' Monographs*, October, 1901, p. 63.

Answer.   The force of the above quotation will be made more clear if we invert it and say that the Elizabethan period was the adolescence of English thought, literature and national life; and that the Renaissance was the adolescence of all Europe, the transition from the childhood of the dark ages to the maturity and enlightenment of the modern world.   The characteristics of adolescence implied in the quotation are the awakening of self-consciousness of the individual, the flood-tide of the emotions, the bursting forth of enthusiasm and imagination, the development of a vigorous will, and the emancipation of the intellect unfettered by tradition and authority—the bulk of freedom of thought

There is (1) a strong tendency toward physical and mental disease, connected with the physical changes of body, brain and nervous system, and toward overstrain at this critical period It is at this stage of life that hereditary tendencies toward abnormal conditions of mind and body begin to assert themselves strongly. (2) A tendency toward morbidity and silliness, on the part of girls; and among boys, toward self-conceit (sometimes self-depreciation) and toward "smartness" especially in the presence of the girls; this tendency being in both sexes the result of the excessive self-consciousness which characterizes the period. (3) A tendency toward mind-wandering and day-dreaming How often the teacher's question has no other effect on the boy than to awaken him rudely from one of these reveries ! How often does he surprise the boy in a painful and embarrassed effort to recall his mind to the topic under discussion before he is made the victim of the derisive laugh of his fellows '

The teacher must remember that there is danger of overstrain—much more frequent among girls, as they are more likely to be over-conscientious,— and lessons must not be assigned so long as to endanger the health and happiness of the pupils.

Under the departmental system, many teachers forget this. On the other hand, the assignment for study must call for vigorous and independent thinking. The period for babying and coddling is past and boys especially must be stimulated to energetic effort, or many of them will sink into a mental lethargy that will be life-long. Further, the teacher must remember that the mind and the will of adolescence must be reached through their feelings. He must get acquainted with the individuality of his pupil, and find out his native interests and capacities, and seek by sympathy and kindness to kindle in him a flame of enthusiasm that will light up not only the pathway of education but of his whole life.

501. Adolescence: elementary and secondary pupils contrasted.—*Mention two important respects in which pupils of the secondary school stage differ from those of the elementary school stage. Show the bearing of this difference on secondary teaching.* (20)

ANSWER APPLIED TO ENGLISH. The secondary school stage is the stage of adolescence. This period is distinguished first, by the dominance of the emotions or feelings, and secondly by the rise and rapid development of reflective reasoning and freedom of thought. This is the period of self-consciousness. Before this, sense of perception, involuntary attention, plasticity of memory, dependence upon authority for guidance, and comparatively weak and transitory emotions, have marked the period of childhood.

The teacher must recognize the fact of the new

life beginning in his class of adolescents; that self-direction and vigorous mental application must begin in earnest; and that the dominance of feeling must be recognized, and that the intellect must be reached through the feelings. The distinction must be vigorous and stimulating, calling for concentrated effort, and still always maintaining the human interest School singing, if rightly conducted, is a valuable instrument for stimulating the healthy emotions School athletics furnish the activity so necessary for the physical development which is fundamental for this period. Literature, perhaps best of all, constitutes the strongest single appeal to intellect, emotions and will. With the child, it is the wonderful that supplies the chain. The romantic, if it exists at all, exists only in embryo. Not so with the adolescent. He has entered into a new world flooded with new thoughts, new imaginations, new feelings, and the impulse toward the romantic is real and cannot be denied And it is in reading literature that these unframed desires and impulses find their expressions, it is the novel and not the Latin grammar that is alive with interest.

Ivanhoe is an excellent example of a book suited to this period. · It seizes upon the feeling with a healthy stimulation, without promoting any sickly sentimentality. It is intrinsically worthy for the intellect, and by its plot and style brings the student into living touch with a real literary masterpiece It furnishes ideals of action and conduct, and so helps to form the will. It provides an interesting basis for the invaluable, but so commonly dull, exercises in English Composition. And Ivanhoe is but a single example of the literary treasures which are open to the students of this period.

Other subjects, excepting, perhaps, natural science in some of the branches, do not exhibit so close a connnection with the native interests or furnish so showy an appeal to the emotions. In these subjects, Latin, for example, the personality of the teacher must form the connection between subject and pupil. A personal interest in the individual student, the faculty of being alive and keeping so, real enthusiasm, kindling a similar flame of enthusiasm in the mind of the pupil, will be sufficient to bridge over the gap, and to bring the student to make earnest effort in mastering a subject which does so great a service both to his knowledge of English and to his processes of thinking.

502. Emulation.—*The Jesuits are adversely criticised for their use of emulation. Discuss its use and abuse.*

ANSWER. No teacher of ordinary experience can deny that emulation is a legitimate factor in the success of every school. Its use by the Jesuits is said to have urged one pupil to perform his task better than another could perform it, and thus a spirit of undesirable rivalry was aroused. Under the sociological view of education, it is held that every student should strive for the welfare of all other students as well as for his own good. In other words, the use of emulation, as applied by the Jesuits, does not harmonize with the modern view of education. Rousseau would not have Emile compare himself with any other children. Emile should compare himself with his own past self and thus have but one standard for progress. James speaks favorably of emulation with one's former self, but he puts a far higher value upon honest rivalry with another. See *Talks*, pages 49 to 54; also Dexter and Garlick, pages 44, 228.

Emulation is justifiably used every time a teacher posts a roll of honor, speaks of individual excellence, writes a letter of commendation to parents, or expresses satisfaction with school work. Emulation is an instinct that yields readily to tact, as all successful teachers know. Its proper use is an effective stimulus.

Misdirected emulation, like other instincts, may lead to evil results. The desire to secure prizes or other artificial incentives is likely to foster dishonesty. In all these matters, the judgment of an experienced teacher is a safe criterion.

503. Suggestion.—*What is meant by suggestion in psychology?*

ANSWER. Suggestion in psychology implies the external substitution of an idea for other ideas in the mind which would follow one another in the natural flow of consciousness. The student sits at his desk in an uncomfortable position. The teacher taps him on the shoulder. He sits up erect. I am sitting at my table. A box of dates is placed before me. The sight of the dates is sufficient to induce me to take and eat. My interest in the book goes on uninterruptedly. The person under hypnotic influence is totally subject to suggestion. He does exactly what he is told. Some educators believe in the power of suggestion to discipline their pupils. Externally forced upon the minds of individuals, suggestion leaves no chance for the development of will. It is sometimes used in the same sense as ideo-motor action where reaction follows immediately upon the presence of the idea. There is this difference, that in ideo-motor action the subject is influenced by objects and not by the interposed suggestion ideas of another.

Suggestion becomes potent in the formation of life habits as soon as a teacher arouses the observing powers of the class. Every pupil gets much from what the teacher says, does and is. The instinct of imitation makes it possible for the largest influences to reach the lives of the children while the direct instruction aims at other benefits. The teacher's penmanship suggests an ideal; the appearance of the desk is another source of imitation; and all the virtues of neatness, accuracy, courtesy, etc., may become effective through the silent suggestion of the teacher's personality. Thus, in a broad sense, suggestion is one of the strongest educative influences.

504. Fatigue.—*Discuss the physical and the psychical aspects of fatigue.*

ANSWER. The answer may follow the line of thought in Dr. LaFetra's article, already cited.

"Prolonged exercise of any set of cells in the body results in fatigue. The cells become drained

of their nutriment, exhausted, and so act with difficulty, if at all. The readiness with which fatigue
of any part will be produced depends inversely both
upon the development of the part and upon the
state of general health. Since the nutriment of
each cell comes from the blood, and since the
amount of nutriment stored up in any cell will depend upon its size, a well-developed muscle in a
healthy, ruddy boy can undergo exercise much
longer before becoming fatigued than a poorly developed muscle in a pale, sickly boy; and the same
is true in the case of brain activity.

"The effects of fatigue, moreover, are noted not
only in the part which has been exercised. A day
of hard lesson produces a tired feeling all over the
body, not simply in the head. This is because the
nerve cells, by their activity, produce waste products, which are gathered up by the blood. These
are irritating and affect the whole body, being carried to every part of the blood. When during repose these products are got rid of, being burned up
by oxidation and eliminated through the skin and
other excretory organs, the tired feeling disappears. During the period of rest, moreover, the
cells recuperate and reload themselves with nourishment from the blood, becoming again plump and
ready for activity. Fatigue which can be readily
dissipated by a night's rest is spoken of as normal
fatigue, or as healthy tire. But if there persists a
tired feeling in the morning after a good night's
sleep, the fatigue is more than normal.

"The amount of study or muscular exercise

which produces simply normal fatigue in a healthy child may produce abnormal fatigue in a child who is physically below par; and if this amount of work is continued the child must have a nervous collapse, or nervous prostration. Children that are the offspring of alcoholic or neurotic parents, those that are anaemic, those that have defects of sight or hearing, those that are growing very rapidly, and especially young girls who are just entering the period of adolescence, are very susceptible to nervous collapse from overwork. Overpressure in schools is most apt to show itself in springtime, after the long winter, when the children have had little outdoor exercise. During this period of the year, moreover, increase in height is more rapid; this always causes great strain on the bloodmaking organs, and so predisposes to anaemia and hence to nervous exhaustion. Mouth breathers and those children who have adenoid growths in the throat are also more liable than others to anaemia and abnormal fatigue.

"Awakening unrefreshed in the morning is one of the early signs of abnormal fatigue. Other signs are inability to concentrate the attention, loss of memory, irritability. If in a more advanced stage, there is morbid introspection and worry, perhaps hypochondria; next, there may be restlessness, diminished sensitiveness, and finally loss of ability to feel tired. Fortunately, the latter symptoms seldom occur in children. One result of over-fatigue is shown by the twitching movements of St. Vitus's dance. When any of the above signs appear over-pressure in school is one of the elements to be thought of as a cause, and the child should be at once relieved of part or all of its school tasks. In writing on this subject Dr. Caille has said: 'The days of brutally whipping children have gone. We are now refined and whip their brains to death.' Children that are convalescent from an illness should be specially guarded against returning to school too soon, as they may develop defects of vision, as well as the general signs of abnormal fatigue."

505. Elective courses.

"Not until the latter part of the high school is reached should there be any latitude in the selection of studies. There is at the present time altogether too much leeway given to boys and girls in this matter. They are not competent to choose what is the best for their own development. Study along the lines of least resistance does not give fibre to the mind; the election of 'snaps' should be discouraged and disciplinary studies required, even up to the university. In fact, it would be well if some kind of disciplinary study could be pursued through life. It is of the utmost importance that boys and girls learn to do well tasks that are not interesting. In life such tasks are constantly arising, and even the most important thing one does may be at the time distasteful."

506. Specialization.—*Show how the elementary school may provide for optional work in higher education.*

ANSWER. A satisfactory point of view is found in Dr. Maxwell's address before the N. E. A. at St. Louis. Four paragraphs follow.

"How is the boy at the age of fourteen to determine what course he shall like? Here is a problem of the first importance, because the boy's future happiness and success in life depend in no small measure on the prudence with which he makes his selection. It is of the first importance to society because there is no economic waste comparable in its proportion to that occasioned by setting people to work for which they have no natural aptitude. I fear we must lay the burden in the first instance on the elementary school—a burden which that institution has hitherto made but little effort to assume. That the elementary school has not done more to guide the future academic work of its pupils is generally atttributed to one or other of two causes, neither of which I believe to be tenable.

"In the first place, it is claimed that the elementary school presents the same subject matter and the same activities to all pupils, and, therefore, turns out a machine-made product, alike in all its parts. The answer is that the elementary school must of necessity present the same subjects and the same activities to all its pupils, because these subjects and these activities constitute the necessary food and the necessary training of the child mind; that the use of the same studies and the same exercises does not result in producing the same type of mind and disposition, because different minds, according to inherent capacities, react in different ways upon the same stimuli; and, finally, that the intellectual capacities, dispositions, and tendencies of the graduates of the elementary schools are actually not alike, but as various as there are individuals.

"The second criticism is that the bright pupil is made to keep step with the dull pupil. The problem really is, not how to drive the bright pupil through the grades at railroad speed, but how to give the slower pupil the assistance—but little will be needed in the majority of cases—that will help over obstacles and enable him to keep up with his more brilliant companions. Any school which lavishes the time and energy of its ablest teachers on the more brilliant to the neglect of the duller pupils falls far short of its duty.

"The fault, then, lies neither in the sameness of the curriculum nor in the retardation of bright pupils, but in the failure of elementary school principals and teachers to realize their responsibility for the future welfare of their pupils. Where, on the other hand, all pupils have equal opportunities and equal advantages, there the teachers, if they take an interest, may note the different reactions produced by identical stimuli on different minds, and advise the boy of literary ability to take the college preparatory course, the one with business instincts to take the commercial course, and the one with a turn for mechanics to pursue the manual training of mechanic arts course. In this way the elementary school may become of much greater benefit to society than it is at present."

Harris on symmetry and specialization.

It is in the first stage, the schools for culture, that these five co-ordinate branches should be represented in a symmetrical manner. On the other hand, a course of university study—that is to say what is called post-graduate work—and the professional school should be specialized. But specializing should follow a course of study for culture in which the whole of human learning and the whole of the soul has been considered. From the primary school, therefore, on through the academic course of the college there should be symmetry, and the five co-ordinate groups of studies should be represented at each part of the course—at least in each year, although perhaps not throughout each part of the year.—*Psychological Foundations*, p. 324.

507. Punishment: defined, approved, not approved.—(*a*) *What is punishment?* (*b*) *Describe and illustrate two modes of punishment proper for use in school; two that should not be used.*

(a) Punishment is the penalty paid for the violation of the rules of conduct.

(b) Private talk in which the teacher aims to place the matter before the pupil as it really is, and the result if such a course is continued. A boy teases a smaller boy on the way to school or on the school grounds. He regards it as fun. His opinion should change after a short, sincere talk with his teacher.

(c) Detention followed by isolation for repeated tardiness, neglect of duty or other wrong-doing. A teacher in our school carelessly left her purse containing a considerable amount in her desk while we were at chapel. She missed it on returning to her room, and it was found in the yard under some leaves, where a boy had placed it until he could safely take it away. It was found that he had been guilty of smaller thefts, and his well-arranged plans in this instance led to his dismissal.

NAGGING.—The unfortunate manner of continually finding fault and ignoring the effort, though feeble, that is made. I know a pupil who is happy this year in her school life because she has been told that she does certain work well—her efforts are appreciated and not overlooked because she is unable to excel in another line of work. She is not continually reminded of her defect.

SARCASM.—A teacher has no right to fling his bad temper at a defenceless pupil in words that ridicule and injure. A teacher of history class in a high school frequently humiliates members of his class by ridiculing their lack of knowledge or their weak expressions. He could use his time more profitably.

Psychology

508. Psychology: history of.—*Outline briefly the history of psychology as a science applied to education.*

ANSWER. See question and answer in section 417.

1. Psychology, in the modern sense of the term, is comparatively a new science. To be sure we have had a so-called mental philosophy since the days of Socrates and Plato. The real psychological movement began, however, with Herbart's attempt to found a psychology upon experience, metaphysics and mathematics.

2. We must come down even to the time of

Weber, Fechner and Wundt to find psychology, even in Germany, established on a firm bases of fact. In England, Spencer, Bain, Lewes, Maudsley and others, all of whose writings belong to the latter part of the nineteenth century, gave form to the movement. In this country, so lately was interest in the new subject awakened that we shall not be far astray if we say that scientific psychology is a product of the last twenty-five years. The first psychological laboratory in America was established at Johns Hopkins University in 1883. The first chair of psychology alone with a laboratory was founded at the University of Pennsylvania in 1888.

3. The two leading periodicals devoted to psychological studies, the American Journal of Psychology and the Psychological Review, were founded in 1887 and 1894 respectively. These facts are sufficient, perhaps, to show how recent in this country was the birth of a really scientific psychology.— Howerth, in *Education*, Nov., 1902, p. 135.

509. Psychology: development.—*What do you consider one of the most valuable results of the modern development of psychology? See 394.*

ANSWER. One of the early results of the psychological movement was a special interest in the development of the child. About 1880, scientific observation of child life began in this country, and rapidly spread until child study became a fad. Both child study and psychology in general began with an intensive study of the psychic life of the individual, and both revealed the necessity of associating the development of the individual with social development. Herbart himself had maintained that "psychology remains incomplete as long as it considers man only as an isolated individual." (1) Vaihinger, Ziller, and other Herbartians advanced the idea that the intellectual development of the individual summarizes the culture of humanity. This idea has expanded into what has been known as the "culture epoch" theory. A brief formulation of this theory may be found in the initial number of Mind, the first English journal devoted to psychology and philosophy, and founded in 1876, in an article by Herbert Spencer on the Comparative Psychology of Man, which concludes as follows: "A right theory of mental evolution, exhibited by humanity at large, giving a key as it does to the evolution of the individual mind, must help to rationalize our perverse methods of education; and so to raise intellectual power and moral nature." Although the theory has been modified, it has done much to direct attention to the relation of education to social development, and has led to the idea, as expressed by Professor Baldwin, that "No consistent view of mental development in the individual could possibly be reached without a doctrine of the race development of consciousness. . . . The relations of individual development to race development are so intimate—the two are so identical in fact, that no topic in one can be treated with clearness without assuming results in the other."—Howerth, *Education*, Nov., 1902.

For criticism of the culture, epoch theory, see Seeley's *Elementary Pedagogy*, p. 77.

510. Psychology and child study.—*Show the importance in psychology of the study of the mental operations of children. Give illustrations of conclusions arrived at from the observation of their words and actions.*

The old idea that children are miniature grown people, only that they require the same kind of instruction in smaller amounts, is fast disappearing. Children are in no sense like grown individuals. The way they think and act is evidence of this statement. The child is the slave of instinct, impulse and blind desire. It takes years of training to cultivate will in the child so that he becomes the master of his animal tendencies. Beneficial instincts, impulses and desires must be fostered, and harmful instincts, impulses and desires must be allowed to die out through disuse. The child has many tendencies in common with lower forms of animal life. His attention flits from one thing to another. He is impressed with things as wholes. He is fearful and shy in strange places. He is the slave of bodily appetites. He loves play. It is the function of child psychology to determine the nature of these child activities, to suggest the best manner in which they can be utilized for further development. The child who calls every man "papa" has not gotten beyond the crude sense-percept. The child who picks to pieces a living butterfly has not gotten beyond the stage where curiosity outweighs sympathy. The child who tells a lie glibly in self-defense does not yet realize the

value of truthfulness to his own conscience and to
other beings. The teacher who does not know the
psychological reason for children's words and actions can't understand why they think and act as
they do. The psychology of the child mind ought
to be a guide to the teacher.

511. Psychology and teaching.

'Education has use for psychology only so far
as it shows the development of mind into higher
activities and the method of such development."

*Discuss this excerpt in the light of your own experi-
ence.*

ANSWER. I say moreover that you make a great,
a very great mistake, if you think that psychology,
being the science of the mind's laws, is something
from which you can deduce definite programmes
and schemes and methods of instruction for immediate schoolroom use. Psychology is a science,
and teaching is an art; and sciences never generate
arts directly out of themselves. An intermediary
inventive mind must make the application, by using
its orginality.—James, *Talks to Teachers*, p. 7.

The Introduction and Chapter I in *Psychologic
Foundations of Education* by Harris will be found
helpful on this topic.

512. Psychology and correlation.—*What is the
comparative weight of psychology in determining the
correlation of studies?*

Psychology holds only a subordinate place in this
determination, the main determination being the
demands of one's civilization,—the duties in the
family, civil society, the state, and the Church.

Next after this, psychology will furnish important considerations regarding methods of instruction. the order of topics as adapted to the pupil's capacity, and the amount of work that such pupils can accomplish.—*Committee of Fifteen*, p. 43.

513. **Psychology, measurement in.**—*How far is measurement possible in psychology? What methods are employed in attempting to measure various kinds of mental phenomena, and with what results?*

ANSWER. In recent years efforts have been made to measure mental operations. Physical measurements are unsatisfactory below the point of stimulation of a sense-organ and above the point of ordinary, normal stimulation. Thus below 16 vibrations to the second and more than 40,000 vibrations to the second the human ear perceives no sound, it matters not how the physical stimulus is manipulated or applied. Within the normal field of stimulation certain proportions in the intensity of stimuli obtain, differing for the different senses. For example, to get a sensation of pressure that differs recognizably from the preceding one the physical pressure must be increased by one-third; to get a sensation of light that is perceptibly different from the preceding one the intensity of light must be increased one one-hundredth. Again, reactions to stimuli will differ just as the person upon whom the experiment is performed is told to *re-act* in an appropriate manner to the stimulus or *to take careful notice* of the exact nature of the stimulus before reacting. The time in the second instance will be considerably more than in the first. The results

are very unsatisfactory when the experimenter tells
the subject to compare one sensation with another,
e. g., whether the succeeding sound is twice, one-
third or one-half as loud as another. The examples
just cited all fall under what are called *quantitive
methods* in measuring psychical processes. The fact
that there is a certain proportion between the intensity of the physical stimulus and a change in
sensation within the field of normal stimulation of
a sense-organ is known as a psycho-physical law.

The other method employed is the qualitative
method. The aim in this method is not to compare
the intensity of two sensations within that realm
of the same sense-organ, but to compare the qualitative difference between two sensations with the
qualitative difference between two other sensations
in the realm of the same sense or of different senses.
For example, the subject is asked to compare the
difference between middle C and D with the difference between E and F. The results obtained by,
this method are quite satisfactory.

514. **Mind: laws of, experiments..**—*What is
meant by laws of mind? How are such laws discovered?
Describe a simple experiment in psychology, indicating
also the aim and the result of the experiment.*

ANSWER. With the consciousness of the individual begin the operations of the mind. In fact, the
mind is but the sum total of consciousnesses of the
individual during his life-time. The way this stream
of thought must flow for every individual gives rise
to the laws of mind.

These laws may be discovered by experiment or

by observation. Experiment differs from mere observation in that the experimenter pre-arranges the conditions under which he looks for specific effects. The mere observer makes no effort to control conditions before looking for effects. The distinction between experiment and observation may be seen clearly in these examples. By mere observation one may notice that the more familiar one is with the contents on a printed page the more easily these contents are assimilated. In experimenting, many pages of printed matter are carefully graded according to the amount of difficulty they offer for comprehension. The results are tabulated with equal care. *The function of experiment is* to establish or disprove the results obtained by observation. Observation is frequently faulty and needs verification or refutation by experiment; e. g., an actor may portray a jovial character and thus appear in a joyous mood to his audience when, as a matter of fact, his heart is filled with grief. Again, observation is more likely to be faulty in psychology than in any other science by reason of such outwardly pretended states of mind. Not only does observation need verification in psychology but even experiment must be verified by introspective analysis, i. e., the individual must examine his own mental processes noting the agreements and disagreements between the results of his introspection and those gained by experiment and observation.

Experiment

I. AIM. To show that the perception of an external object is determined by apperception as well as by sensation.

II. DESCRIPTION. (1) Education is a science. (2) Look at sentence (1.) What do you see at the first glance? Do you really see "Education is a science," or would it not be nearer the truth to say that inter-changing black and white surfaces make different impressions on the retina of your eyes? If your perception consisted of pure sensation could you designate the stimulus as black and white?

III. RESULT. At first I seem to see "Education is a science." By observation I know that the illiterate whose eyes are just as perfect as mine could not see such a sentence. By introspection I know that if I could not read and did not know white from black, the stimulus could not appear as white and black to me.

IV. CONCLUSION. The perception of an external object is determined by apperception (the contribution the mind makes to the effect of the stimulus) as well as by sensation (the direct effect of the stimulus).

515. Mind: faculties; objections to faculty theory. —*State some of the leading classifications that have been made of the fundamental operations of mind. What is meant by a mental faculty? Discuss the objections which have been made to the use of this term in psychology. What are the methods of study open to the psychologist?*

ANSWER. The usual classification of mental operations is Intellect, Feeling and Will. Some of the forms of intellect are sensation, perception, apperception, memory, imagination, association, and reason. Feelings, or emotions, are designated as anger, fear, love, joy, sympathy, etc. Will includes impulse, appetite, desire, etc. According to the phrenologists, Gall and Spurzheim and their followers, these different mental operations had a particular location on the surface of the brain. One's fortune was told by feeling the bumps on the cranium. Subsequent investigations have shown that the mind is a unit. None of these different manifestations, known as faculties, is separated from the others. They are all parts of the same thing, mind, only showing the different phases of the same unit. The term faculty when it implies one of the divisions into which the mind is supposed to be divided is a misnomer. If you destroy intellect, you destroy feeling and will. There is no thought or act in which these three elements are not present, though they may not be present in equal proportions. The simple process of solving a problem in arithmetic involves the knowing what you want to solve, the desire to do so, and the actual attempt.

The methods upon which the psychologist bases his knowledge of the different manifestations of mental operations are: (1) The biological comparison method in which he compares the nervous system of man with the nervous systems found in lower forms of animal life; (2) the method of experimental extirpation in which certain parts of the central nervous system are cut out in the lower forms of animal life and the effects noticed; (3)

the method of mechanical stimulation and irration in which case parts of the brain are pricked with a sharp instrument, or an electrical current is passed through them and the effects noticed; (4) the natural decay of the nervous system noticed in post-mortem cases and comparing these nervous changes with the changed actions which took place as a result of these cases of paralysis; (5) the histogenetic-method which noticed the development of the central nervous system during the various stages of its development. This is the least satisfactory because its validity depends upon post-mortem examinations of individuals at the various stages of development.

History and Principles of Education

516.   According to nature: meaning, corollaries. —(*a*) *What do you understand by the statement, "We must proceed according to nature"? (b) Give three educational corollaries based on this principle, stating how each corollary is or may be applied in school work.*

ANSWER. (*a*) To Rousseau, "Proceeding according to nature" meant to return to nature, to get away from books, to live close to the plants, streams, trees, etc., to get away from the conventionalities laid down by society and be free once more. To Comenius, "Proceeding according to nature" meant to conduct the educational process as you plant seed. Begin in the spring-time. Make the conditions favorable, etc. But Rousseau, Comenius, Pestalozzi and Froebel had another meaning for the expression, "We must proceed according to nature," and this is the present educational view. It means that we must proceed according to the nature of the child. We can't teach the child percentage or proportion before his mind is ready to grasp it. The missionary can't convert a heathen by preaching abstract sermons to him on truth, service, loyalty, etc. He must approach the abstract by personal, concrete examples of these virtues,—truth service, loyalty, etc. So the child, to know number in the abstract, must first count and measure things.

(*a*) Corollaries.

1. Go from the simple to the complex. Show that 1 is contained into 2 twice before asking how many times ½ is contained into 2.

2. Experience before rules or definitions. Show by having pupils examine carefully a sufficient number of sentences that adverbs modify verbs, adjectives or other adverbs before asking them to formulate a definition..

3. Proceed from the known to the related unknown. The child knows common fractions. Take up decimals which are only another form of fractions expressed with different symbols.

517. Locke: treatise, views, criticism.—(*a*) *What treatise did Locke write on education? For what immediate purpose? (b) Name two general points on which he laid great stress. (c) Give with reasons, two of his suggestions which you think wise, and two which you think unwise. (d) Name a writer on education who was influenced by Locke, and state one respect wherein he was influenced.*

ANSWER. (*a*) Locke's treatise, *Thoughts on Education*, was written for the advice of a friend.

(*b*) 1. His scheme of education concerned primarily the sons of gentlemen, not the children of the masses. As he believed that virtue and good manners were more important than the acquisition of knowledge, he strongly advocated instruction by a private tutor in preference to the schools of his day, because he thought that in the schools the boy would be influenced rather by his fellows than by the master, and so fail of attaining a high standard of good breeding and moral character.

(*b*) 2. Physical education, so long neglected, was one of the points on which Locke laid the greatest stress. "A sound mind in a sound body," was his idea of education. He would educate for life, not for the university.

(*c*) 1. *Wise suggestions.* His suggestion that punishment should be mild and reasonable, that the spirit of the child should not be debased and enslaved, that the child should be reasoned with in the matter of conduct, has become the sound educational doctrine of our day and needs no defense. Such is the theory of discipline followed in this city and it has proved successful in practice. We are educating reasonable beings to think and act for themselves; future citizens to govern themselves. The mere suggestion of flogging a boy to-day for a failure in construing a Latin sentence would be sufficient to render the teacher liable to examination by an alienist.

(*c*) 2. *Wise suggestions.* He further recognized

the principle that there are certain seasons of
aptitude and inclination on the part of the pupil;
that the mind cannot act in season of depression;
that the teacher should never attempt to force the
balky will, but lead and stimulate the mind by interest. This also is sound doctrine to-day. The
teacher who enters into a contest of wills and tries
to compel the accomplishment of a certain task,
say after school, by the sheer exercise of authority, finds himself and the boy both injured, and his
purpose defeated. In such a contest as this, often-
times the boy *cannot* learn. His mind is dazed and
cannot act, and the fault lies largely at the teacher's door. Let the teacher be sympathetic and encourage the boy; let him try to guide and lead and
stimulate; let him seize upon the boy's times of
alertness and mental activity, and he will not have
to do any driving.

(*c*) 3. *Unwise suggestions.* Locke's views on
physical education, sound in the main, are open to
just criticism where he advocates the "hardening
process." As Herbert Spencer says, "Many children have been hardened out of the world." Scant
clothing, perforated shoes and wet feet and irregular meals are condemned as much by educators, at
least since Herbert Spencer wrote on physical education, as they are by the medical profession. The
reasons are obvious.

(*c*) 4. *Unwise suggestions.* Locke's advocacy
of education by private tutors rather than in the
schools has not been approved by subsequent educational practice. He overestimated the direct in-

fluence of the private tutor in forming the mind and character of his pupils, and underestimated the indirect influence of the masters of the school. The boy is as likely to copy the weaknesses of his tutor —and tutors are not infallible—as his strong points. Again, the moral atmosphere of many a school is determined largely by its masters, e. g., Dr. Arnold of Rugby. Further, admitting that the standard of morality of the average schoolboy is not high, Locke failed to catch the point that the growing boy must *needs* be influenced more by the fellows than by his elders, just as in after life he will be influenced chiefly by his associates of the same age. The gulf in age and interests between a boy in his teens and his tutor—Rousseau recognized this fact—is too great to be easily bridged On the whole, then, it is better for a boy to be educated in school with his fellows than to be sheltered and coddled under the wing of a private tutor.

(*d*) Rousseau was influenced by Locke in the direction of physical education. Emile must grow up a physically perfect young animal.

518. Plato, Comenius, Jacotot, Spencer, Rousseau, Milton.— [*Answer only two of the following five points.*] *State the views* (*a*) *of Plato on music in an educational scheme;* (*b*) *of Comenius or Jacotot, on the proper method of teaching a language;* (*c*) *of Spencer, on the place in education of the study of literature and art;* (*d*) *of Rousseau, as to discipline;* (*e*) *of Milton, as to the proper scope of education.* (16).

(b) Jacotot was a French educator of the early

part of the 19th century. His method of teaching a language was largely based on his maxim "All is in all." He used Fenelon's Telemachus as the text-book. This was memorized by his pupils, and so thoroughly mastered that all the pupils needed to know of grammar, rhetoric, etc., was based on this one piece of literature. In fact, he believed that all knowledge of philosophy, history and mathematics could be taught by using the Telemachus as a center, thus emphasizing the principle of correlation. Repetition was another principle of his method. His maxim or paradox "One can teach a language not known to him" was based on his own success in teaching Dutch children the French language, they being entirely unacquainted with that language and he having no knowledge of the Dutch, by using the Telemachus as above described.

(d) Rousseau, a French educator of the 18th century, believed in the discipline of natural consequences. That is, he believed that the best way to discipline a child and teach him the difference between right and wrong, was to let him suffer the natural consequences of his wrong-doing as punishment. For example, when Emile broke a window, he was compelled to stay in the room and suffer from cold; when he did not perform his tasks, he was obliged to forego the food that would have been secured through the performance of his tasks These punishments were to appear to Emile as the natural and unavoidable result of his own wrong act.

519. Realism and naturalism.—*Explain meaning and show relation to method of teaching.*

As has been said, the latter part of the 16th century witnessed an educational movement in favor of the study of real things. For many years the study of Latin and Greek was the chief means of education. Rabelais and others objected to the study of Latin and Greek because they said that such study was a mere memory process based upon words. They directed attention to the study of natural objects and thus made the beginning of a movement known as realism in education. The movement continued during the succeeding years and it has broadened to include all forms of nature, human and otherwise. The name naturalism became associated with the movement in the 18th century. Naturalism implies subject-matter and methods of teaching in accordance with the requirements of human nature and external physical nature.

520. *Give the basic justification for the prominence of language studies in the course of study. See Report of Com. of Fifteen.*

The justification is found in the fact that language is the instrument that makes possible human social organism.—Page 44.

521. *Summarize the suggestions of the Committee of Fifteen in regard to the criticism of words rather than things in elementary education.*

Place more stress on the internal side of the word, its meaning; and use better graded steps to build up the chain of experience and the train of thought that the word expresses.—Pages 45-46.

522. *What is the specific value of technical grammar?*

Technical grammar can never devlop a higher and better English style. Only familiarity with fine English works will insure one a good and correct style. The chief objective advantage of grammar is that it shows the structure of language, and the logical forms of subject, predicate and modifier, thus revealing the essential nature of the thought itself, the most important of all objects, because it is self-object. On the subjective or psychological side, grammar demonstrates its title to the first place by its use as a discipline in subtle analysis, in logical division and classification, in the art of questioning, and in the mental accomplishment of making exact definitions.—Page 48.

523. *Do you advise the use of literary masterpieces for the purpose of parsing in technical grammar?*

No. Four or five years in the practice of grammatical analysis, practice on literary works of art (Milton, Shakespere, Tennyson, Scott) is a training of the pupil into habits of indifference, dread and neglect of the genius displayed in the literary work of art.—Page 49.

CHAPTER XV

SETS OF QUESTIONS WITHOUT ANSWERS

524. For estimating self.—These three sets of questions are enough to enable a student to judge himself in relation to capacity for adaptation. Failure to answer all the questions is considered (*a*) lack of knowledge, or (*b*) lack of executive fitness. Why called executive?

Examination in 1906. *Time, 2 hours.*

525. Give the meaning of the following: suggestion, attention, imagination, apperception, renaissance, humanism, realism. (21).

526. (a) What is it to generalize?

(b) What is the use of generalizing?

(c) What are the chief obstacles to correct generalizing?

(d) How, in your specialty, may the power to generalize be developed? (16).

527. Enumerate the conditions under which habits may be most effectively formed. Illustrate from high school work. (16).

528. "The interpretation of education from the point of interest is as partial as the old interpretation of education as discipline. * * * The present tendency is one of reconciliation, or harmonization, or interest and effort, as a basis of educational practice."

(a) Show that these two interpretations are partial.

(b) Show how they can be reconciled

(c) Show from high school work in your specialty

529. Discuss the following:

"The world is still governed by sentiment, and not by observation, acquisition, and reasoning; and national greatness and righteousness depend more on the cultivation of right sentiments in children than on anything else."—President Eliot

530. Give a brief account of any two of the following

The Academy of Athens.

Monasticism.

The work of Charles the Great for education

Jesuit schools

English "public schools."

The report of the "Committee of Ten."

Examination in 1908

531. (a) What is habit?

(b) State two principles underlying habit (6)

(c) Show how these may be applied to your specialty (6).

532 (a) Define reasoning

(b) State in the form of general rule how pupils may be trained to reason

(c) Illustrate the application to your subject (15)

533. (a) What is "mind wandering?"

(b) What are the causes?

(c) How may it be overcome? (12)

534. State various purposes for which questioning is used in teaching. (15).

535. By what means is attention in class secured when but one pupil at a time is making recitation? (12).

536. (a) State difference between inhibition "by repression" and "by substitution." (16).

(b) Apply to high school discipline.

537. Give four rules (maxims) to bear in mind when assigning advanced lessons. (15).

Examination in 1910.

538. All nervous centers have then, in the first instance, one essential function, that of intelligent action. They feel, prefer one thing to another, and have "ends." Like all other organs, however, they evolve from ancestor to descendant, and then evolution takes two directions, the lower centers passing downwards into more unhesitating automatism, and the higher ones upward into larger intellectuality.—James.

Define and illustrate meaning of nervous centers, lower centers, higher centers, intelligent action, automatism. (15).

539. Education is the superior adjustment of a human being to his environment.—Horne.

(a) Explain this definition, especially environment.

(b) What part does your speciality play in this environment. (15).

540. The greatest word in education is Interest.
—Schurman.

(a) Discuss this statement.

(b) Explain the part of interest in your specialty (or how you would get interest in your specialty). (24).

541. Discuss the use of incentives in high schools. (15).

542. State and illustrate four common mistakes in questioning before a class, and illustrate how to avoid each. (16).

543. Describe briefly one of the following:
Socratic Teaching.
Work of Comenius.
Rousseau's Emile.
The Chapter on Intellectual Education in Spencer's *Education*. (15).

CHAPTER XVI

QUESTIONS FOR WRITTEN ANSWERS

544. There is but little assured value in any educational course for teachers unless such teachers make a practical application of the theories which they will advocate as approved modes in the education of children. Self-activity, apperception, reaction, self-realization,—these will remain vague concepts unless students utilize their own motor activities in writing. The following questions are offered, therefore, as worthy tests of your effort.

545. Define education.

546. Name seven ideals in the history of education. Which one is the most comprehensive? Give reason for your choice.

547. Define and illustrate correlation, co-ordination, concentration, and enrichment as applied to a course of study..

548. Describe the Socratic method and state its limitations.

549. Give advantages and disadvantages of the topical methods. Illustrate by using your specialty.

550. Briefly discuss general method under these headings:

1. Meaning..
2. Justification.
3. Limitations.
4. Application.

551. What is the meaning of each of the following terms as applied to education:

(a) Spencer's *complete living;*

(b) Herbart's *many-sided interest;*

(c) Dewey's *social stimulus;*

(d) Pestalozzi's *generation of power;*

(e) Butler's *inheritance of the race?*

552. What practical help may be drawn from the culture epoch theory?

553. (a) Define interest in the educational sense. (b) Enumerate five ways of securing interest in school organization, i. e., developing a good school spirit. (Consult *Methods in Education,* abbreviated M., p. 54).

554. Voluntary attention is a power developed by many acts of attention,—the result of habituation. Tell how you present a lesson in your specialty in accordance with this opinion.

555. Three laws underlying habit are plasticity, motive, regular repetition. Show bearing of these laws on teaching a specified topic. Mention five kinds of drill to secure accuracy in your specialty.

556. In speaking of training the memory, we have the terms apprehension, retention and reproduction; association by similarity and contiguity. Illustrate the first three in teaching. State the law of contiguity.

557. Explain inhibition by repression, inhibition by substitution. Apply to cheating on examination.

558. Name five school virtues that should be substituted respectively for five school vices, and explain your method of inhibiting by substitution.

559. What is your interpretation of the term general method? Show how it embodies the inductive-deductive method, method-whole, from particular to general, and from concrete to abstract. What is its relation to the apperceptive process?

560. Explain and illustrate (*a*) apperceiving mass or group, (*b*) reaction in psychology, (*c*) artificial incentives.

561. Define apperception.

562. Induction, deduction and analogy are mentioned under kinds of reasoning. State briefly the specific uses of each.

563. (a) What do you understand by the statement, "We must proceed according to nature"? (b) Give three educational corrollaries based on this principle, stating how each corrollary is or may be applied in school work.

564. Define habit.

565. Jacotot said: "All human beings are equally capable of learning. Everyone can teach; and, moreover, can teach what he does not know himself."

Discuss this quotation briefly. Quote your own experience as reasons for your opinions.

566. Give arguments for and against the assignment of home study.

567. Much is said about habituation to right thinking and willing. Show its application (*a*) in teaching punctuality; (*b*) in teaching pupils how to study; (*c*) in overcoming cheating on examinations.

568. What is the relation between attention and interest? Mention five of your devices to arouse and sustain interest in the recitation.

569. Mention, with reason, three specific values of the study of your specialty.

570. "American teaching in school and college has been chiefly driving and judging; it ought to be leading and inspiring" (*President Eliot*). Give, with reasons, your opinion as to the truth of these two statements, illustrating each kind of teaching. Show how teaching can be made to conform to the ideal stated.

571. Outline the arguments for manual training in the elementary schools, under the heads (1) value to the individual, and (2) value to society.

572. Discuss the educational value, and name the main principles of the kindergarten; or sketch the history of the manual training movement.

573. Explain and illustrate the following terms:
(*a*) Visualization.
(*b*) Verbal memory.
(*c*) Constructive imagination.
(*d*) Connotation of terms. (16).

574. (*a*) Describe three symptoms of brain fatigue in children. (6).

(*b*) Give, with reasons, three ways for avoiding such fatigue. (6).

575. Explain any two of the following:

(*a*) The place of music in Greek education (including the meaning of the term music).

(*b*) Froebel's ideas of development and his principle of self-activity.

(c) Herbart's doctrine of interest.

576. Give at least two principles governing promotion of pupils.

577. (a) Define punishment. (b) What are the advantages and the disadvantages of natural punishment?

578. Define abstraction, socialization, adolescence, suggestion, motivation, self-realization.

579. Distinguish instructing, teaching, educating, functioning.

580. "Every faculty during the period of its greatest activity is capable of receiving more vivid impressions than any other period."—Spencer.

Express in a statement—

(a) The principle implied in the expression, "Every faculty during the period of its greatest activity." (1).

(b) Illustrate this principle from the development of a child in the elementary school period; in the high school period. (10).

(c) Mention two educational corollaries that may be drawn from the principle. (10).

581. (a) What is meant by the cultivation or development of the power of observation? (5).

(b) Show, by giving directions and illustrations, how the power of observation may be developed or trained—

(1) In general; (5)

(2) In your specialty. (5)

582. "In each branch of instruction we should proceed from the empirical to the rational."

Explain and illustrate. Give reasons for rejecting this principle. (20)

583. Give, for each of the following, two important and distinctive principles regarding education enunciated by him: (20)

Herbert Spencer,

John Locke,

Friedrich Froebel.

584. (*a*) What is habit? Illustrate. (*b*) Mention two important conditions that tend to fix
habits. Illustrate. (*c*) Mention one advantage of
habit, and one disadvantage. Illustrate.

585. "Rabelais, Montaigne, Locke, Rousseau
form a succession."

(*a*) Give reasons for this statement, naming two
important principles which these writers held in
common.

(*b*) Name one distinctive feature in the educational theory of each. (1)

586. "It is due to a * * * prejudice, inherited from antiquity, against these arts (i. e., the
material or manual arts) that their great educational value has not been seen. This value is threefold: * * * "—*Thomas Davidson.*

(*a*) Discuss the view presented in the first sentence of the quotation.

(*b*) What do you understand to be the threefold educational value of these arts?

587. All instruction must be individual instruction. To teach a class is to teach the individuals
composing it, and not some substituted abstraction.

It is possible to form a class so that the needs of each member may be as fully met as if each had his own teacher. Quite a wide range of ability, especially in upper classes, is consistent with individual instruction in classes. Absolute uniformity is necessary only for those teachers who force pupils to square-inch text-book results; but the teacher who puts flexible and living problems to the class may engage strong pupils to their utmost capacity, while the weakest work to advantage.— Tompkins, *Management*, p. 112.

Can class instruction and individual instruction be distinguished? Interpret the excerpt and then criticise it favorably or adversely.

588. "The * * * High School period is the period in which the transition is made from boyhood and girlhood to manhood and womanhood, when new feelings and interests are awakened and come with a kind of surprise, when both youth and maiden find themselves in a new world, for which their training and habits have hardly prepared them, and in which, therefore, they are most liable to go astray, unless proper precaution be taken. The leading characteristics of all the studies of this period should be vigor, calling for a strong exercise of will, and a good deal of energetic emotion."—Thomas Davidson.

Explain and discuss the two points in this quotation briefly giving your own view of the characteristics of pupils in the High School period, and of the work to be done in it.

589. "Mere verbal statements, made and heard as such, do not constitute real teaching in any subject. * * * Real teaching aims at the development of mind in relation to the subject matter."— *Bryant.*

(*a*) Give a reason for the truth of each of these statements. (6)

(*b*) Explain the second statement with illustration. (10)

590. (*a*) What is the meaning of the term "judgment" as used in psychology? Illustrate. (*b*) What is meant by "good judgment" as the term is commonly used? (*c*) Give two illustrations of the developing of good judgment in school, explaining how good judgment is developed in each case.

591. Describe and illustrate the teacher's use of the principle of logical association of ideas for fixing knowledge in the memory. (15)

592. "The teacher must think of his subject not a body of facts to be acquired, but as a mental habit or attitude to be cultivated."

Discuss this dictum, explaining the terms used. Illustrate its application to your specialty.

593. (*a*) Describe the manner in which the mind forms general concepts, illustrating from your specialty. (15)

(1) State three conditions to be borne in mind by the teacher as aids in the formation of general concepts. (15)

594. "Education is the process of making individual men participators in the best attainments of the human mind in general; namely, in that which is most rational, true, beautiful and good."—*Whewell*.

"The educational end, as I conceive it, might now be stated thus: Right judgment, and a habit of good action under a sense of duty, accompanied by a comprehension of the spiritual significance of nature and man."—*Laurie*.

(*a*) Contrast these two statements in respect to their point of view. (7)

(*b*) Briefly explain and illustrate each of the following terms as here used: (1) Right judgment. (2) (2) A habit of action under a sense of duty. (2) (3) A comprehension of the spiritual significance of nature and man. (2) (*c*) Criticise, with reasons, any point in either section. (7)

595. Distinguish instinct and habit. Make a list of eight instincts to be observed in educational work.

596. Define definition. (See logic).

597. What is meant by intention of terms and extension of terms?

598. Illustrate logical division or classification.

599. Define fallacy, mediate inference, logic.

600. What is the relation of habit to education?

INDEX

www.ingramcontent.com/pod-product-compliance
Lightning Source LLC
LaVergne TN
LVHW012205040326
832903LV00003B/139